Activating the Untapped Potential of Neurodiverse Learners in the Math Classroom

All students deserve access to a rich and meaningful math curriculum. This book guides middle and high school teachers toward providing all learners – including neurodiverse students – with the support necessary to engage in rewarding math content. Students who receive special education services often experience a limited curriculum through practices that create long-term disadvantages and increase gaps in learning. The tools and strategies in this book help teachers better understand their students to move them closer to their potential. Chapters include differentiation, assessment, classroom structure, and learning targets. Both general education math teachers who have not been trained in special education support and special education teachers with a limited background in standards-based math pedagogy will learn new skills to improve their teaching from this practical resource.

David Johnston taught middle school for 17 years and is certified in both math and special education. He has also worked as an instructional coach supporting and training math and special education teachers across several campuses. This book developed out of his work as a teacher, coach, and professional development leader. He is currently pursuing a PhD in Curriculum & Instruction from Texas Tech University.

T0386434

Activating the Untapped Potential of Neurodiverse Learners in the Math Classroom

Tools and Strategies to Make Math Accessible for All Students

David Johnston

NEW YORK AND LONDON

Designed cover image: © Shutterstock

First published 2024
by Routledge
605 Third Avenue, New York, NY 10158

and by Routledge
4 Park Square, Milton Park, Abingdon, Oxon, OX14 4RN

Routledge is an imprint of the Taylor & Francis Group, an informa business

© 2024 David Johnston

ISBN: 978-1-032-38693-5 (hbk)
ISBN: 978-1-032-38545-7 (pbk)
ISBN: 978-1-003-34633-3 (ebk)

DOI: 10.4324/9781003346333

Typeset in Bembo
by MPS Limited, Dehradun

Contents

Part I

Introduction

Introduction

Each student comes into our classroom with a unique combination of skills, interests, backgrounds, and needs. We try to construct a classroom environment that accommodates each student and allows them to thrive. Some of our students require an extra level of support, and it is our professional responsibility to provide the support outlined in a student's Individual Education Plan (IEP). A student's IEP is a treasure trove of information, and it unlocks access to a wealth of support for both the student and the teacher. The IEP identifies academic, social, and/or functional goals and describes strategies to help students reach those goals. In the best circumstances, an IEP represents an agreement between the student, educators, and caregivers to provide services that will help the student develop and increase in independence.

As teachers, we strive to learn about our students and learn about support strategies to facilitate our students' growth. As we continue to learn, we adjust our classroom practice, and hopefully, our students benefit from our growth as teachers. It seems there is always more to learn, and it's important that we continue growing, for our students' sake. Let me share a story about some shifts in my own classroom practice and a particular former student.

I used to let my students in my classroom sit wherever they wanted.

Because I didn't know any better.

I quickly realized that was not the most effective teaching practice. I had earned an undergraduate degree in mathematics, but my math content knowledge did not prepare me with all the necessary pedagogy skills to teach math to middle school students. Imagine my shock when I discovered that 12-year-old 8th graders do not always make decisions in accordance with their best educational outcomes. But I learned better. Through my graduate night classes, I learned about concepts like the power zone, heterogeneous grouping, and visibly random seating. I started rearranging my classroom seating and my students' learning improved. One of my mentors told me struggling learners often choose to sit in the back. So, in my second year in the classroom, I used a system on the first day of class to randomly seat all of my students toward the front of the room, leaving the back row empty.

DOI: 10.4324/9781003346333-2

It worked great, but only on the first day of class. My fancy system meant that any students who started after the first day – students with schedule changes, late enrollers, or students who were absent – had to sit in the back because those were the only empty seats. Some of those students were the ones who needed the most support, and I had inadvertently placed them together at the back of the room.

I needed a new system. After my second year, I intentionally left empty seats scattered around the room while still seating students toward the front. When students arrived on day two (or day five), I could assign them an empty spot, and they didn't have to sit in the back.

Then I met a student named Raquel.

Raquel was an 8th grader. She received special education services, and her Individual Education Plan (IEP) listed goals in math calculation and reading comprehension. She was placed in English and math classes where co-teachers were present daily for additional support. Raquel lived with extended family, and her school attendance was spotty. When Raquel entered my classroom after missing the first week of classes, I was proud of myself for planning ahead. I applied my clever seating system and gave her a choice of two empty desks, each about halfway toward the back of the classroom.

I didn't notice, but while the class was working, Raquel had discreetly taken her paper, moved out of her seat, and stood over a file cabinet at the side of the room. She quietly did her math work there, using the file cabinet as a sort of table while she stood.

This was not what I – nor my clever seating system – had anticipated. Initially, my co-teacher and I weren't sure what to do, so we just went along with it. We checked on Raquel, giving her help and direction when she needed it. Over the next several days, she usually worked at her same file cabinet. She would engage in group work and talk with her peers, but when it came to independent work, she went back to her standing workplace. I thought if I ignored it, Raquel would eventually move to a desk. She didn't, but she got her work done, so we worked with her.

I had helped raise children in my home who received special education services, but even that experience had not fully prepared me to teach math to students like Raquel. Instead, I learned through more professional development, a few books, some graduate courses, and plenty of conversations with case managers and special educators – as well as learning from my mistakes in the classroom. My co-teacher and I made the decision to allow Raquel to work where she wanted because of our knowledge and experience working with struggling students. Raquel had experienced several years of academic failure and needed to exert some control over her environment. We intentionally designed student choice into many of Raquel's assignments to increase her feeling of ownership over her learning. My co-teacher and I had previously encountered students with physical and social issues that make it challenging to sit and work with groups. Even though Raquel's IEP didn't indicate these same issues, we knew she had moved schools frequently and issues like these might not have been observed or documented. We alerted her case manager, but in the end, it seemed like a minor accommodation to allow her to work outside of her seat.

Raquel had a few other quirks. She struggled in math, but my co-teacher and I were able to help her make some real progress during the school year. Raquel didn't always get along with everyone, and she ended up in the office from time to time, but I felt her experience in our math classroom was very positive.

Her experience in other classrooms was not the same.

In Raquel's English class, she tried to find a place where she could stand and work, but her English teacher wouldn't tolerate it. He expected every student to sit in their assigned seat until they had permission to move somewhere else. This would quickly turn into a power struggle. Raquel would be sent to the hall and eventually sent to the office. Where my co-teacher and I were willing to accommodate Raquel's seating (standing) preference – even though it wasn't mentioned in her IEP – her English teacher would not make that accommodation. And while Raquel would do math work while standing at a file cabinet, she did not complete any English work sitting in the principal's office.

Raquel's case manager made some adjustments to her IEP, but despite those efforts, Raquel had very different educational experiences in these two classrooms. I respect Raquel's English teacher, and I'm sure he had reasons for making the classroom decisions he made. The number of students in the classroom or the dynamic between certain students may have made it difficult to accommodate Raquel's seating preferences. I suspect he was trying to establish clear classroom procedures and implement a uniform policy for all of his students.

I honestly believe Raquel's English teacher – like most teachers – wanted to see all of his students succeed. Like all of us, he was doing the best he could in that situation with the tools, training, and experience he had. I know my experience with Raquel better equipped me for the next time I experienced a similar student, and I hope her English teacher felt the same way.

If you have already been a classroom teacher, you can probably think of a student like Raquel – someone who needed special accommodations. Maybe you were able to meet their needs, or maybe you needed to reach out to get help from peers, case managers, special education coordinators, or academic coaches. As you read this book, think about the needs of those students. Think about their specific cognitive abilities and how they impact learning. Consider the planning necessary to meet their specific needs and address their unique IEP goals. Reflect on the instructional and testing accommodations that would benefit their learning. Ultimately, the goal of this book is to help you take the information, tools, and strategies listed here and use them to help individual students.

Teaching math to students with IEPs requires an extensive skill set. It also requires the help and support of several staff members. As you build your skill set, I also encourage you to build your network of support. No one has all the answers, but we should never stop looking and learning.

1 What We Believe about Teaching Math to Neurodiverse Students

Each classroom contains a diverse population. Students come to our schools with a wide range of cultural, linguistic, and social backgrounds. Some students speak several languages. Others have extensive travel experience. Each of their households is unique. We also see extensive physical diversity among our students: I've seen 6th graders who look like they could play varsity football and high school seniors who look like they just left elementary school. There is just as much neurodiversity inside our students' minds as there is physical, cultural, and social diversity on the outside. Our students are each unique in the way they process information, the speed at which they work, or the mental connections they make between academic concepts.

For some students, this neurodiversity is sufficient to qualify for special education services. These students will have Individual Education Plans (IEPs) describing specific academic, social, or functional goals that teachers will support throughout the school year. There are guidelines and legal requirements to follow when educators provide services to students with IEPs, but many of the skills and strategies we implement for this population will make us better teachers for all the students in our classrooms. All our students exhibit neurodiversity, and it is important for all teachers to learn to support the neurodiversity found in their classrooms.

Teaching math to secondary students with IEPs draws on two distinct skill sets: math pedagogy and special education pedagogy. This chapter guides the development of those skill sets by exploring the purpose of math instruction, our beliefs about teaching students with IEPs, and the ways special educators and math educators can collaborate to build effective instruction together.

The Role of Math Instruction

As students are gaining unprecedented access to knowledge and resources, teachers are challenged to prepare them for an ever-changing future. Many of today's math teachers work in schools that look and feel very different from the schools they attended as students. Many of them learned math in a very different

DOI: 10.4324/9781003346333-3

setting from the math classrooms we see today. And often, the goals of today's math classrooms contrast sharply with the classroom goals of 20 years ago. Clarifying the goals of secondary math instruction will help guide the rest of our work: how we communicate to students, what types of lessons we create, what topics we assess, and how we respond when students struggle.

I invite you to consider your math classroom goals for a moment. What do you hope to accomplish with your students this year? Imagine it is the end of the semester or the end of the school year. How will you determine if this year's class was successful? What are the skills or accomplishments you hope your students will exhibit at the end of your time together? Take a moment and jot down some answers on a sticky note or in the margin of this page.

When I work with teachers one-on-one, I love hearing their answers to this question. I feel it gets at the heart of their reason for working in the classroom. Teaching is a demanding profession, and our answers to this question often remind us why we tolerate challenges. When teachers tell me their definition of success, they tend to focus on the big picture. They share their hopes for their students' futures. They almost never talk about annoying behaviors or standardized test scores. In fact, their responses tend to fall into four categories. As you read these categories and their descriptions, see if your own response was similar.

- **Understanding** - I often hear teachers talk about helping their students develop number sense. They want their students to fluently work with numbers and understand when an answer is reasonable. Some struggling learners enter our secondary math classrooms after experiencing years of failure. Often, we start measuring success by simply building confidence. We want to help students take some risks and believe in their ability to perform quality math work. Several teachers tell me they want their students to overcome their math phobia before the school year is complete. Often, a large part of overcoming math phobia is understanding the math they encounter. As math becomes less about following a list of steps and more about understanding relationships, students can better make sense of their work.
- **Problem Solving/Application** - Teachers sometimes tell me their students know a lot of arithmetic but don't know when and how to use it. One common category of classroom goals is helping students to apply their math skills and become effective problem solvers. This is especially appropriate in secondary math classrooms where the focus shifts from concrete arithmetic skills to abstract reasoning skills.
- **Tools and Resources** - We understand we cannot always be there to support and guide our students. They must become more independent as they prepare for future coursework and life beyond school. Some teachers aim to provide students with mathematical tools, strategies, and

resources they can continue using in the future. They want to empower students to seek help on their own when they need it so they can take control of their own learning.

- **General Growth** - Teachers sometimes list other areas of general growth. We hope our work impacts students and we strive to help them change for the better. Teachers often describe areas they want their students to improve and grow over the course of a year: more persistent in their math work, more confident in their abilities, better communicators and team members, making progress toward IEP goals, or closing performance gaps.

The National Council of Teachers of Mathematics (NCTM) (2018, 2020) defined their position on the role of secondary math instruction. In doing so, they recommended goals for the math classroom. In a sense, the council's recommendations represent their definition of a successful school year. NCTM stated the math classroom should help students:

- Develop a deep understanding of math
- Prepare for future professional opportunities
- Use math to analyze the world around us
- Appreciate the joy and beauty of math

Consider how these recommendations fit with your own vision for your math classroom and your students' success. These goals should apply to all students – not only those in advanced classes or those planning to attend a four-year university – these are the purposes of math instruction for each and every student. That includes students who receive special education services.

This book attempts to combine knowledge of math pedagogy with knowledge of effective instruction for students with IEPs. The view of math instruction centers on this list of beliefs:

- Math instruction should help students make sense of the world around them.
- Math curriculum should balance procedural knowledge with conceptual understanding.
- Math teachers should integrate effective teaching practices such as developing student discourse, connecting multiple representations, and promoting problem-solving.
- All students deserve access to rich and meaningful mathematics.

First, we want our students to understand how the math they are learning relates to the world outside of school. This makes the content more engaging for students (and preempts the "when will we use this" question), but it is also pragmatic. As teachers, we are not teaching skills simply because they will be on the next test. We teach topics to benefit our students in the long term.

This means students need to understand math concepts at a deeper level. It is not enough to copy a problem from the board and replicate the teacher's work through several practice problems. Students should understand, for example, why a certain relationship should be modeled with a linear equation instead of a quadratic equation. They should have some ideas about estimation and reasonableness. They need to know when to apply the skills they have learned. The math we encounter outside of school is not usually arranged in neat columns that match the example at the top of the page. Real-world math requires more flexibility and fluency.

Students with IEPs need to form the same relationships. Teachers want to prepare all students for life outside of the classroom. For students with IEPs, teachers may use different tools to help build understanding. Graphic organizers or manipulatives may be necessary to help students develop the deeper understanding we desire or to understand how to connect the math they learn with the real world.

Next, we want math instruction to balance conceptual understanding with procedural calculation ability. Both procedural and conceptual knowledge play a vital role as students learn mathematics. Correct solutions will always be important, but we delight in hearing students use correct reasoning to explain their work. This balance between procedural calculation and conceptual understanding shifts as students move into secondary math. As students leave elementary school, there is less focus on arithmetic and a greater focus on application and reasoning. Our secondary math classrooms are designed to prioritize thinking, teamwork, and understanding over speed and rote calculation. As a result, we rarely see timed tests. Instead, we see open-ended questions that ask students to explain their reasoning or describe why a particular answer is wrong. We see more calculators and computers in secondary classrooms as the emphasis shifts away from basic arithmetic.

It may be appropriate for some students with IEPs to have a different procedural/conceptual balance than their peers. If a student struggles with math calculation, for example, teachers can identify areas of strength that students can leverage to solve problems despite weakness in calculation ability. For some students with IEPs, procedural calculation may focus on reasonableness and estimation to evaluate an answer instead of the process of calculating a result.

Further, there are effective instructional strategies each secondary math classroom should implement. NCTM (2015) identified Eight Mathematics Teaching Practices, describing effective teacher actions in the classroom. These are practices such as: connecting mathematical representations, emphasizing problem-solving and reasoning, and developing academic discourse among students. These practices not only build strong mathematicians but also reinforce 21st-century skills, such as communication, collaboration, and critical thinking. As teachers implement these practices in the classroom, they are preparing students for future math work and success outside the classroom.

These are skills that all students require – including students with IEPs. NCTM's Mathematics Teaching Practices can often be used to support student IEP goals in many content areas. As students grow in reasoning and communication, they will also develop their ability to self-advocate since they can effectively describe their current understanding and where they need additional help.

Finally, this approach to math instruction is grounded in equity and access. All students deserve access to rich and meaningful math instruction. We do not reserve critical thinking and problem-solving for a few students in specific courses. We make sure all students have opportunities to engage in problem-solving at their current level of understanding. Whenever it is appropriate, students with IEPs should have access to the same curriculum as their peers. This means whenever possible, engaging in grade-level content, the same level of rigor, and similar learning outcomes.

Instruction for Students with IEPs

Math is an integral part of any student's secondary education – including students who receive special education services. Today's math curriculum encompasses much more than arithmetic, and the math classroom provides an opportunity for teachers to help address a wide range of students' IEP goals. Addressing IEP goals – and supporting students with IEPs in general – requires intentional planning. This work is guided by research, training, and experience. This book is written with the following perspective regarding instruction for students with IEPs:

- Instruction should build on students' strengths.
- Teachers should emphasize high-impact content.
- All students can engage in rich, meaningful mathematics, with the appropriate support.

There are varying viewpoints regarding special education services. This book takes an asset-based approach that perceives the variation in student abilities as a natural part of human diversity. If a student exhibits an academic weakness – perhaps below average ability to hold information in working memory, difficulty with reading comprehension, or challenges with math calculation – this is not viewed as a defect to be cured. Rather, teachers can help students identify areas of strength that students can leverage to compensate for areas of struggle. In the secondary math classroom, for example, teachers may intentionally design practices to strengthen students' understanding or teach students to use resources such as manipulatives, graphic organizers, or calculation aids to overcome areas of challenge.

Teachers should intentionally prioritize learning targets for students with IEPs to emphasize essential skills that will benefit students in the long term.

Struggling math students often need extra time to master skills and concepts. This can prevent students from covering the same number of learning targets as their peers. Therefore, instruction should focus on high-impact math concepts and skills students will continue using in future coursework or skills that can be applied in multiple areas. Specialized topics with limited applicability should be reserved until students have mastered more essential content.

Students with IEPs should be afforded access to the same rich, meaningful math as their peers. All students should have opportunities to practice procedural skills and develop their reasoning and problem-solving abilities. This may mean teachers need to provide scaffolds to make rich math tasks more accessible. Students with learning gaps can still participate in meaningful math work with the appropriate support. This approach supports student equity, helps students close learning gaps more quickly, and improves student engagement.

Bridging Two Worlds of Pedagogy

Students with IEPs need support from qualified math content teachers and from trained special educators. General education math teachers and special educators each possess essential knowledge and experience to help students overcome educational barriers and meet their potential. Some secondary campuses partner teacher pairs in a co-teach relationship where two teachers are in the classroom sharing responsibility for a classroom of students. In other instances, math teachers may consult with special education teachers or case managers to plan instruction and support for students with IEPs. Regardless of the arrangement, general education teachers and special education teachers need to communicate with each other, sharing their own knowledge and experience to create the best educational plan for the student.

Math teachers bring their content area knowledge and an understanding of math pedagogy. General education teachers know how topics in the current curriculum fit within the broader vertical alignment of math content connecting across grade levels. They are familiar with the prior knowledge students will need, and they can anticipate potential learning gaps that teachers will need to address. They also recognize the connections between current classroom topics and future math coursework. This helps teachers prioritize learning by emphasizing the skills students will need for future success.

In addition to this content knowledge, general education math teachers understand the broader goals of modern math instruction. They are trained in teaching conceptual understanding of math concepts and developing problem-solving and reasoning skills. Math teachers have experience using student-centered approaches to develop math knowledge by building on students' strengths. Students with IEPs should have access to the same curriculum as their peers whenever appropriate, and the general education teacher is the math curriculum expert.

Special education teachers are typically the most familiar with sources of student challenges, potential barriers to learning, and effective accommodations to overcome those barriers. They can provide guidance in helping students make progress toward IEP goals and collecting data to measure that progress. Typically, special educators are trained in a wide range of skills, including assessment, instructional strategies, and collaboration with peers and student caretakers. These professional skills are essential in providing the necessary support to students with IEPs.

The Council for Exceptional Children (CEC) (2017) defined 22 High-Leverage Practices for special educators. The set of practices relating to instruction dovetail well with NCTM's Mathematics Teaching Practices and extend them to support students with IEPs. Special education teachers can collaborate in the design of instruction and adaptation of tasks to meet specific learning goals. Their expertise extends past content area instruction to also include social and behavioral skills as well as a variety of cognitive abilities such as memory, listening comprehension, or visual processing. Special education teachers are well situated to collaborate with general education teachers to develop scaffolded supports to help students reach learning goals.

The collaboration between general education and special education teachers is a vital component of Specially Designed Instruction (SDI). SDI is the essential component of special education services, and it should be provided to every student with an IEP (Friend & Barron, 2021). SDI is purposeful, documented, planned instruction designed to address students' IEP goals. SDI also integrates a plan to help students become increasingly independent. Teachers should always keep in mind that special education services are more than scaffolds and supports; it is intentional instruction to help students progress toward specific goals. This instruction is unique to each student's IEP and relies on effective collaboration between general education teachers and special educators.

Using this Book

Teaching is a cyclical process as teachers design lessons, deliver instruction, and assess student learning. This book is organized according to three general segments of the lesson cycle:

- **Before Instruction Begins** - This section describes teacher actions before students enter the classroom. This includes becoming familiar with students' needs, identifying learning goals, and anticipating differentiation.
- **During Instruction** - These chapters address teacher actions while working with students. There are strategies for grouping students, tips for using manipulatives or graphic organizers, and suggestions for monitoring student learning in real time.

- **After Instruction** – This portion of the book discusses the steps teachers take before restarting the lesson cycle. Teachers need to assess student learning, analyze data, and make plans for students who need further instruction.

Each chapter addresses a specific component of lesson design, delivery, and analysis. The chapters can be read independently in any order. Teachers or learning communities can read the book linearly or skip to chapters focusing on specific areas of instruction. I hope this book will provide valuable resources, and I also hope it will be a launching point for further learning. I encourage you to discuss these ideas with your professional network and share your knowledge and experiences. Above all, remember that each student is unique. Special education services are guided by students' *Individual* Education Plans. There is no single set of answers to address the needs of each *individual* student, but as teachers, we continue to support each other as we work together to meet all students' needs.

References

Council for Exceptional Children. (2017). *High-leverage practices in special education: Foundations for Student Success*. Council for Exceptional Children.

Friend, M., & Barron, T. (2021). *Specially designed instruction for co-teaching*. Marilyn Friend, Inc.

National Council of Teachers of Mathematics. (2015). *Principles to actions: Ensuring mathematical success for all*. NCTM.

National Council of Teachers of Mathematics. (2018). *Catalyzing change in high school mathematics: Initiating critical conversations*. NCTM.

National Council of Teachers of Mathematics. (2020). *Catalyzing change in middle school mathematics: Initiating critical conversations*. NCTM.

Part II

Before the Instruction Begins

2 Student Strengths, Needs, and Goals

Special education services cover a wide range of student characteristics. The Individuals with Disabilities Education Act (IDEA) identifies 13 different categories of qualification. It is not unusual for students to qualify for services under multiple categories, but some characteristics are much more common than others. The IDEA categories most frequently encountered in the general education setting include Specific Learning Disability (SLD), Speech or Language Impairment, and Autism. The relative frequency of each IDEA category is shown in Figure 2.1 (National Center for Education Statistics, 2021).

The largest category, comprising about one-third of students who receive services, is SLD. Local education agencies vary slightly in how they identify SLD, but in general, it is a condition where issues with the student's basic cognitive abilities impact specific academic areas such as reading comprehension or math calculation. This chapter will explore the more common cognitive abilities and how they impact learning in the math classroom. Many students who receive special education services can be successful in secondary math classrooms, though they may need specific support. An understanding of IDEA categories and the underlying cognitive abilities will allow educators to tailor instruction to meet the specific needs and abilities of students with IEPs.

IDEA Areas of Disability

Twelve of the IDEA categories of disability apply to secondary school students. Each student is unique, and these conditions may manifest differently in different students. The brief definitions that follow provide general descriptions (IDEA, 2004).

- Specific Learning Disability: Describes a condition where a student's academic progress is impacted by difficulties in one or more cognitive skills. This is the most common category of students who receive special education services. Common sub-categories of SLD affecting students' math ability are

DOI: 10.4324/9781003346333-5

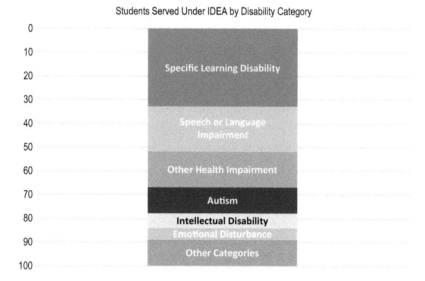

Figure 2.1 This graph shows the percentage of students receiving special education services according to their primary category of IDEA disability. Categories not
displayed account for less than 2% of the population of students receiving
services.

math calculation and math reasoning. The category of SLD includes dyslexia
and excludes learning problems that fit within the other categories of IDEA.

- Speech or Language Impairment: Challenges with communication, for
  example, stuttering, which negatively impact a student academically.
- Other Health Impairment: Issues related to strength, energy, or focus that are
  due to chronic health problems and negatively impact a student's academics.
  This might include attention deficit hyperactivity disorder.
- Autism Spectrum Disorder (ASD): A persistent condition impacting social
  interaction, communication, and sensory processing. ASD often manifests in
  intense interests or repetitive behaviors.
- Intellectual Disability: A severe impairment to intellectual development, such
  as Down Syndrome.
- Emotional Disturbance: A persistent mental health condition that negatively
  impacts a student's academic performance. This may include anxiety,
  depression, bipolar disorder, or other issues.
- Multiple Disabilities: Students may be classified under multiple categories of
  disability, but the category of "multiple disabilities" indicates that a student
  exhibits characteristics of multiple conditions that align in such a way that
  traditional services for individual conditions would be inadequate.

- Hearing Impairment: This category includes deafness. This is a severe loss of hearing and is separate from the cognitive ability of auditory processing.
- Orthopedic Impairment: Conditions such as cerebral palsy that impair physical function.
- Traumatic Brain Injury: Brain injury caused by external injury or accident.
- Visual Impairment: This category includes blindness. This is a visual impairment so severe that it cannot be corrected. This is separate from the cognitive ability of visual processing.
- Deaf-Blindness: This category describes students who have a combination of severe hearing and vision impairments. This combination has such a profound impact on communication that special services are necessary beyond those that are provided for deaf or blind students.

These categories and their definitions are revised over time. These general descriptions reflect amendments to IDEA up to 2017.

Cognitive Abilities

Specific Learning Disabilities (such as math problem-solving or math calculation) describe what challenges a student may experience in class, but they do not identify the cause of those difficulties (Cormier et al., 2017). Two different students could exhibit the same SLD, but for different reasons. Just as we do not expect a doctor to treat all coughs with the same prescription, a teacher cannot effectively support all students with a given SLD in the same way. Consider three fictitious students who each have an SLD in the area of math calculation:

- Alex struggles with math calculation because they have below-average working memory. Alex is only able to hold small amounts of information in working memory, and as a result, they often lose track of their progress when performing math calculations.
- Dylan's processing speed is slower than their grade-level peers. They require more time to perform even simple arithmetic calculations. Often when Dylan realizes they are falling behind their classmates on a task, they begin rushing and making careless mistakes in their work.
- Hunter has challenges with visual processing. Because they have trouble processing visual information, they are prone to errors in calculation, particularly when they need to line up columns of numbers, such as when they are multiplying multi-digit numbers or adding a long list of numbers.

A teacher may observe that each of these students has similar struggles performing math calculations, but each student would benefit from different supports. Alex may be successful using a multiplication chart or learning estimation strategies so they can check the reasonableness of their answers. It might be adequate to provide Dylan with a working environment that is free of distractions so they are not comparing their progress to their classmates. A teacher might also consider shortening Dylan's assignments and tests. Hunter may find it useful to solve problems on grid paper or work on assignments that provide extra white space.

It is important to note that the examples in this chapter are simplified narratives. Cognitive abilities often manifest differently in individual students, and each student has a unique combination of strengths and weaknesses in each cognitive ability. Each student's brain works in its own unique way, and special education services are tailored to the needs of the individual.

Knowing details about each student's cognitive abilities can help teachers understand the cause behind each student's SLD. Cognitive abilities are the processes in the brain that control how an individual takes in and uses information. There are many cognitive abilities, but psychologists and special educators often focus on a few high-impact areas such as fluid reasoning and crystallized intelligence. Students' cognitive abilities are often measured when they are initially assessed for special education services. It may be helpful to understand some of these cognitive abilities and how they impact academic performance in the math classroom. This is an active field of research, and the terms for these cognitive abilities will vary over time, but these categories describe several of the factors that influence students' development of math skills and reasoning.

Crystallized Intelligence

The knowledge and skills a student acquires over time are referred to as crystallized intelligence. This may include previously learned vocabulary, formulas, or symbols. An individual's crystallized intelligence typically expands over time and allows them to apply their knowledge in familiar situations. When we encounter students with below-average crystallized intelligence in the math classroom, we may notice that – when compared to grade-level peers – they exhibit behaviors such as:

- Confusing symbols such as *greater than* or *less than*.
- Struggling with related terms such as mean, median, and mode.
- Choosing the wrong math operation because they focus on noticing the presence of specific words such as "total" or "more" instead of how the words are used in a problem.

Fluid Reasoning

Fluid reasoning describes a student's ability to apply their knowledge in a novel situation. When learners encounter a new type of problem, they typically use reasoning skills to apply their current knowledge and experiences to the new situation. This includes identifying ways in which the new problem is similar to and different from those problems they have encountered in the past. Students who struggle with fluid reasoning in math class may display:

- The ability to perform a calculation (like dividing or squaring a number) but not recognize when to apply the skill in a problem.
- Difficulty connecting related concepts such as the Pythagorean Theorem and the Distance Formula.

Short-Term Working Memory

When a learner temporarily holds information in their brain, they are utilizing their working memory. The information is not stored long-term in this case. Students can typically hold 3–5 items in working memory. If math students have working memory challenges, the teacher may notice them:

- Struggling to complete simple mental computations like multiplying by two or adding 10.
- Skipping steps in a problem or forgetting what a problem is asking and not working all the way to the solution.
- Copying notes or instructions one word at a time.
- Struggling with multi-step problems.

Long-Term Retrieval

Separate from working memory is the ability to store and retrieve items from long-term memory. While working memory includes the ability to temporarily hold information and work with it mentally, long-term memory is a student's ability to retrieve the information they learned previously. When teachers encounter a student who seems to need to re-learn a skill after a few days or weeks though their peers still demonstrate mastery, this may be the result of issues with long-term memory and retrieval. Students with long-term retrieval issues in the math classroom may:

- Freeze-up when asked to recall information (like formulas or procedures) on demand.
- Perform poorly when assessed in pressure situations.
- Struggle to recall previously learned information.

Visual Processing

Visual processing is a student's ability to make sense of visual information. This does not describe a vision impairment, but rather how well a student can take in and use diagrams or written information regardless of the quality of their eyesight. Visual processing is a high-impact skill in secondary mathematics. Students compare data visually, use visual models to represent fractions and ratios, use visual estimation strategies to verify geometric calculations, and much more. If a student's visual processing ability is below their peers' they may:

- Struggle to identify attributes of geometric figures such as obtuse or acute angles.
- Exhibit difficulty representing values on a number line or visually estimating ratios.
- Be challenged when interpreting visual graphs such as pie charts or bar graphs.

Processing Speed

Each student is different and many students work at their own pace. The measure of how quickly a student can reason, analyze information, and respond is processing speed. This seems to be a larger factor on math performance in lower grades where the focus is often on skill acquisition. As students move into secondary grades, they begin applying their skills and working with more complex math tasks. Processing speed is often deemphasized at this point as instruction focuses on reasoning and application and students have tools to assist with simple arithmetic. In math class, issues with processing speed may mean a student:

- Completes less of their independent practice in class, increasing their homework load or resulting in less opportunity to work under the supervision of a teacher.
- Lags behind their peers when completing tests or tasks.
- Requires more think-time when learning new information or considering the answer to a question.

Each student in a classroom (not just students who receive special education services) will have strengths and weaknesses in each cognitive ability. Students may have weaknesses in multiple cognitive abilities, and those areas will interact to impact the student's classroom performance. Knowledge of a student's cognitive abilities is just one information source to help when planning instruction and support.

IEP Goals

Each student who receives special education services will have an Individual Education Plan (IEP) describing their area(s) of need and setting goals for their progress. Even though the details may vary between states and districts, students with IEPs often have at least one goal for each area in which they exhibit

Table 2.1 Sample IEP math goals. A student's IEP goal(s) typically describe the condition when the student's progress will be measured, the behavior or skill the student is developing, and a measurable level of performance

---

When presented with a grade-level problem-solving task, Hunter will accurately use a strategy to create a plan to solve the problem in 4 out of 5 attempts during the grading period.

Evan will correctly select which math operations to use when solving a multi-step word problem 80% of the time.

Ryan will use a calculation aid to accurately multiply decimals when using a formula to solve a problem in 4 out of 6 attempts during the grading period.

---

a need. Students may have multiple math goals as well as goals in reading, language, or behavior.

IEP goals should serve as a guide for the student's Specially Designed Instruction (SDI) which is described more fully in Chapter 1. The student's SDI should provide strategies and practice directly aligned to help students progress toward IEP goal(s). Some sample IEP goals related to math skills are contained in Table 2.1.

IEP goals may look very different even on the same campus, but these examples all contain three common components: a context that describes when the goal behavior is happening ("when presented with a grade-level problem-solving task," "when using a formula to solve a problem"), the desired behavior ("correctly select which math operations to use," "use a calculation aid to accurately multiply decimals"), and a measurable target ("4 out of 5 attempts during the grading period," "80% of the time").

A student's IEP goals and SDI do not make up the entire curriculum, but it is an important focus for teachers who serve students with IEPs. As teachers are providing content instruction, they should identify opportunities to address students' IEP goals and provide SDI within the structure of the class day. This may be a small group or one-on-one instruction, an accommodated task, supplemental support, or other instructional strategies tailored to the student's developmental need.

Math teachers should be aware of all their students' goals – not just their goals related to an SLD in math. Modern math classrooms feature rich questioning, academic discourse between students, and written and verbal reflections on learning. Many of these typical classroom activities use skills related to SLDs such as Listening Comprehension, Written Expression, Oral Expression, or Basic Reading Skills. When teachers are aware of these goals, they can anticipate the challenges that students will encounter. The example in Table 2.2 illustrates how common math classroom activities can be leveraged to support students' IEP goals.

Table 2.2 This typical classroom task can be used to address several IEP goals

Classroom Task

At the beginning of class, students study the following "Which One Doesn't Belong" prompt.

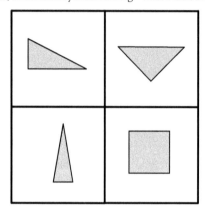

After some independent processing time, they take turns sharing with a partner which image they believe does not fit with the others and explain their reasoning.

Potential Related SLDs

Oral Expression - Students may struggle to verbalize their reasoning to a partner, particularly without adequate time to prepare.

Listening Comprehension - This task requires students to listen to their partner's reasoning, which may be different from their own. It may be difficult for some students to process the explanation their partner shares verbally.

Processing Speed - Some students will take more time to compare and contrast the four images in this prompt. The open-ended nature of this task can have a paralyzing effect on students who are not yet used to the freedom of responses this task provides.

Math Reasoning - Depending on the source of a student's math reasoning difficulties, this task may contain obstacles to student learning. Students with poor visual processing may not notice that some shapes have right angles while others do not. Students will need to draw on their crystallized intelligence to describe the differences between these images and explain their reasoning to a partner.

Potential Scaffolds

Depending on the specific students' strengths, some of these scaffolds may be adequate to allow a struggling student to engage in this task:
- Preview - allow a student to view the prompt in advance of the other students. Perhaps the prompt can draw from images that were used in a previous assignment.
- Sentence Stems - provide prompts to begin student conversations. "I noticed one of the shapes is different because … " "Looking at the angles, I noticed a shape that is different is … " "Only one of the shapes is named … "

(Continued)

Table 2.2 (Continued)

- Extended Practice – allow students to listen and share with different partners more than once so they can refine their thinking and practice organizing their thoughts.
- Simpler Problem – remove one level of the task by assigning one image and asking a student to explain why it doesn't belong. "Tell your group how the square is different from the other shapes."

Again, this is a simplified example that does not capture the complexity of a student's neurological, academic, and behavioral issues, but it does show how important it is for math teachers to be familiar with a student's entire IEP. The IEP and its goals are a valuable tool to help teachers better understand their students' needs and help teachers identify opportunities to help students gain greater independence.

Identifying Student Strengths

Effective math instruction will leverage students' strengths and use them to extend content skills and knowledge. For example, if a student is struggling with visual processing, they may have difficulty arranging fractions in order using diagrams (Figure 2.2).

Fortunately, there are other methods to arrange fractions in order. Students with strong calculation skills could convert the fractions to decimals or find equivalent versions with common denominators. Some students may be able to compare the given fractions with benchmark values. The task may still be challenging, but teachers can identify which route the student has the best resources at their disposal. As students build up their facility, they can add to that strength as they make connections to other concepts and skills.

Arrange the fractions $\frac{4}{9}$, $\frac{2}{6}$, $\frac{3}{4}$, and $\frac{3}{7}$ in order from least to greatest.

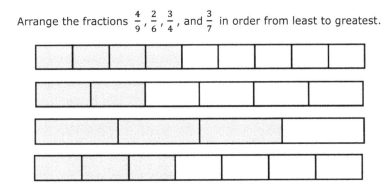

Figure 2.2 For students who struggle with visual processing, diagrams such as these may not help them observe the comparisons between fractional parts of a whole.

The student's IEP and case history should provide insight into what strategies have been effective in the past. Teachers should review each student's IEP and discuss with campus personnel (such as the student's case manager) any pertinent information in the student's evaluation for special education services. Each student in our classrooms has unique strengths and weaknesses in each cognitive ability. If a student has been evaluated for special education services, someone has already identified several of those strengths and weaknesses. This is valuable information that helps teachers understand their students and plan for their success.

References

Cormier, D. C., Bulut, O., McGrew, K. S., & Singh, D. (2017). Exploring the relations between Cattell–Horn–Carroll (CHC) cognitive abilities and mathematics achievement. *Applied Cognitive Psychology, 31*(5), 530–538. 10.1002/acp.3350

Individuals with Disabilities Education Improvement Act of 2004, 20 U.S.C. § 1400 et seq. (2004).

National Center for Education Statistics. (2021, February 2). *Digest of Education Statistics, 2020.* National Center for Education Statistics (NCES) Home Page, a part of the U.S. Department of Education. Retrieved January 4, 2023, from https://nces.ed.gov/programs/digest/d20/tables/dt20_204.30.asp

3   Student Readiness

If you have watched a middle school or high school basketball game, you have noticed the varied skills and abilities of the players on the court. There is usually a significant range of heights and builds, as well as ball-handling ability, speed, and awareness of the game. Coaches tell me that some years they have a group of players that can execute sophisticated plays, and some years their team needs a simplified game plan. I am always impressed with athletic coaches who can understand the ability and potential of the players on their team and create a game plan suited to their team's strengths. Those coaches often have very different styles of gameplay each year depending on the strengths of specific team members.

The math classroom features just as much diversity in ability and readiness. Students in a single classroom are of different ages. They have different language backgrounds. They begin the year with a wide range of experiences from prior math classes. Some have moved between schools several times, while some have benefited from family support or tutoring outside of school. As much physical diversity as we see on the basketball court, there is likely even more internal neurodiversity in our math classroom. It is not reasonable to expect that this diverse group of students will be ready to learn the same math lesson, in the same way, on the same day. This is one of the reasons we develop Individual Education Plans for particular students: they have unique needs, and teachers need to be aware of them to help students reach their goals. Diversity of math readiness is not limited to students with IEPs, however, effective teachers implement strategies to identify where students are now and help them develop the skills they are ready to learn next.

This chapter will provide some tools for measuring student readiness and look at how the knowledge of student readiness fits into instructional design. To meet the needs of more learners, teachers need to use their knowledge of student abilities to differentiate the classroom.

A primary reason for gauging student readiness is to increase student engagement. If the class content is not challenging enough, students can easily become bored. They do not see the value in the material they already know or

DOI: 10.4324/9781003346333-6

material that develops too slowly. Students with attention or impulsivity issues may begin finding other things to engage their interest. As students strengthen their skills and knowledge, teachers have to increase the rigor and challenge of instruction or students will become less engaged (Paige & Neace, 2013). Similarly, if students do not have the prerequisite skills to engage in classroom tasks, they will become frustrated and disinterested. This can have a long-term impact as students form their own perceptions of math and their ability to successfully participate in a math class. Many students with IEPs have spent multiple years feeling like they could not meaningfully engage with their peers in math class. Eventually, they may become intimidated by math, they may believe the problem is within themselves, or they may divert attention from their struggles with negative behaviors.

Vygotsky (1978) addressed the importance of matching instruction to students' current readiness when he defined the Zone of Proximal Development. The most effective learning happens when students are challenged to learn content just slightly ahead of their current ability. Teachers design learning experiences and facilitate learning to build on students' current skills and stretch their thinking just a bit further. Mastering this balance, however, first calls for understanding students' current abilities and level of understanding.

Pre-assessment

Teachers can benefit from having advanced knowledge of their students' strengths and areas where they are likely to struggle. This helps teachers anticipate where to prepare support or extra practice. It can guide teachers as they design instruction to build on students' current knowledge. It is not always feasible to gather this kind of information. If pre-assessment is not implemented carefully, it can be time-consuming for students to complete and for teachers to analyze. It may also not provide the specific information teachers need. There are methods of pre-assessment that can give teachers a clearer picture of their students' level of readiness. Whenever possible, pre-assessment should be short, focused, and strengths-based.

Pre-assessments should usually use a short list of questions that students can quickly complete. Pre-assessment is intended to inform teachers as they are planning instruction. It would be counterproductive for the pre-assessment to take up large amounts of class time that can be better spent on instruction. A long pre-assessment will not only use up class time, but student performance tends to drop off as tests get longer. As testing fatigue sets in, teachers will get a less accurate picture of their students' abilities. Instead, poor performance may be a result of attention issues or stress. Many students exhibit reading or memory issues that require extra time. These effects will be exaggerated on longer tests. In most cases, several shorter pre-assessments will provide more accurate information than a single long pre-assessment will.

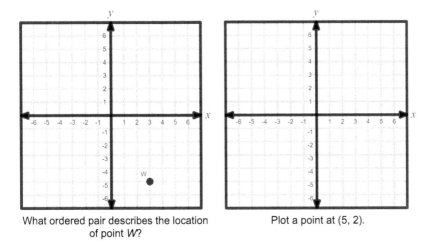

What ordered pair describes the location of point *W*?

Plot a point at (5, 2).

Figure 3.1 This short pre-assessment allows a teacher to quickly identify students who need to review prior skills before a lesson about transformations in the coordinate plane. The pre-assessment gauges whether students are able to plot and identify ordered pairs, a necessary skill for creating transformations.

Figure 3.1 shows an example of a short pre-assessment for a teacher to use prior to a lesson about transformations on the coordinate plane. The lesson requires students to create transformations by manipulating ordered pairs using addition or multiplication. This will require students to plot ordered pairs and identify the ordered pairs that describe specific points on the coordinate plane. The example pre-assessment in Figure 3.1 will allow a teacher to identify any students who need to review identifying and plotting ordered pairs.

This example pre-assessment uses two questions to efficiently determine whether a student is reasonably fluent with the use of ordered pairs. It is not necessary to ask several questions about points in all four quadrants. The teacher is just checking for a prerequisite level of familiarity. The questions are not multiple choice in order to get a more accurate picture of students' abilities. Students cannot guess answers for these questions but must show their true level of understanding. Since the pre-assessment is two short questions, the teacher can still efficiently gain the information they need without resorting to the use of multiple-choice questions.

Next, pre-assessments should focus on the specific skills teachers need students to use in upcoming lessons. Secondary math encompasses a wide range of skills. Successful students apply logical reasoning, geometric knowledge, reading ability, arithmetic skills, proportional reasoning, and much more. This makes it difficult to succinctly describe a student's math ability. The same student who reads and understands math text at a level similar to 6th-grade peers may exhibit proportional fluency on par with 8th-grade students. As teachers measure their students' readiness through pre-assessment, they should focus on exactly the skills they want to measure.

Pre-assessments should be short, and they should also be focused. This means it may be necessary to conduct multiple pre-assessments throughout a unit as teachers need to learn about student readiness on a variety of skills or topics. This can be accomplished by using warm-up questions at the beginning of class or exit tickets at the end of class. Teachers can capture these short opportunities to gather data for planning future lessons. The process described in chapter 4 for developing learning targets can also be used to identify specific student skills for pre-assessment.

Finally, pre-assessments should be structured so that students can experience some degree of success. As much as possible, we want pre-assessments to be a positive experience where students can show off what they already know. Teachers need to learn about students' abilities as well as any potential gaps. It is important to help students understand the role of pre-assessments. They are intended to help students by identifying areas of need. They are not intended to hurt students by dropping their grades. In fact, it would generally be inappropriate to use a pre-assessment as a graded assignment since it covers prerequisite material that has not been taught in the current class.

In the example from Figure 3.1, notice students were asked to plot a point in Quadrant I. This is usually the quadrant where students are most comfortable. A student's performance on this task tells teachers what they need to know. If a student cannot plot a point in Quadrant I, then review or intervention is necessary.

By contrast, if the question had been more difficult, for example, "Plot the point $(-3.5, 2)$," it would have provided less information. If a student could not plot this point, located in Quadrant II, a teacher would not know if the student struggled with the negative value, the decimal, or with all ordered pairs. The original question is more accessible to students and more informative to teachers.

One strengths-based pre-assessment that requires little teacher preparation is the protocol *Tell Me Everything You Know*. This task consists of the teacher posting a prompt about an upcoming topic. Students are asked to spend two minutes writing down everything they know about the topic. This task is so open-ended that every student can usually write something meaningful, and fluent students can also show off the depth of their knowledge. There is no advanced preparation necessary. The teacher simply announces the topic for students to write about. For example, "Tell me everything you know about parallel lines," or "Tell me everything you know about compound events."

As you can see in the examples in Figure 3.2, teachers can easily gauge an individual student's level of fluency with a particular topic. These student responses to the prompt "Tell me everything you know about the y-intercept of

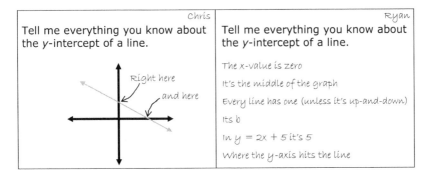

Figure 3.2 These sample student responses to a "Tell me everything you know …" prompt illustrate how teachers can gauge a student's level of readiness based on their response to an open-ended question.

a line," demonstrate how the task adapts itself to each student's level of understanding and gives the teacher a clear picture of their readiness.

In the sample student responses shown in Figure 3.2, Chris seems to believe that the *y*-intercept is any place where a line crosses either axis. This is a clear misconception, but the teacher can see exactly what to address. Ryan, on the other hand, seems to understand several aspects of the *y*-intercept. Their reasoning lacks some academic vocabulary, such as "vertical," but Ryan lists some important aspects of the *y*-intercept. Each student was able to answer this question at their own level, and the teacher received valuable information to use when planning future instruction.

Pre-assessing student knowledge is a valuable step in preparing lessons and differentiating instruction. It is important to use pre-assessment effectively to gather accurate data and keep students engaged. By designing short, focused pre-assessments that reveal student strengths, teachers can gauge student readiness without sacrificing instructional time.

Prerequisite Knowledge

Pre-assessment will often reveal gaps in students' prior knowledge. However, not all knowledge gaps require the same amount of attention. Cathy Martin (2020) suggests dividing prior skills into three categories depending on their priority for future learning. Teachers can address each of these categories differently.

Essential Concepts for Upcoming Instruction

This is foundational knowledge that students will need before they can meaningfully engage with future lessons. For example, if students are learning about the volume of rectangular prisms, it is necessary that students understand what the area of a rectangle represents. If there are students in the class who have gaps related to calculating the area of a rectangle, the teacher can plan a short review or intervention specifically on that topic.

Specific Information for Today's Task

This represents information that is necessary for a particular lesson, but it is not necessarily an essential conceptual understanding. For example, if students will be determining the volume of cereal boxes, they will need to know how to use a ruler to measure length. Students can certainly still learn about volume, even if they do not know how to measure with a ruler. However, early during this task, the teacher would probably check in on specific students and demonstrate how to use the ruler for this task.

Just-In-Time Knowledge

This is factual information that teachers can quickly pass along to students right as they need it. For example, if students are calculating the volume of cereal boxes, as the teacher reads the instructions, they may stop and clarify that the word *dimensions* describes the measurements of the box, in this case, the length, width, and height.

The modern math curriculum contains so much information that it is difficult to cover it within a school year. This task becomes even more insurmountable when teachers also cover prior years' material in order to address gaps in student learning. It is essential, therefore, for teachers to address learning gaps by the most efficient means possible. This means teachers should identify exactly which students have which specific gaps. Teachers should use whole-class reteaches only in rare circumstances. Instead, it is important to tailor reteach lessons to specific groups of students and implement them in stations or small groups.

Accessibility

Students with IEPs will often exhibit learning gaps. Their teachers are constantly working to help students access grade-level content despite those gaps. Math students constantly build on their prior skills and knowledge, but that does not mean all math content must be mastered in a linear fashion. Students with gaps in Algebra can still master Geometry. Students who continue to struggle with arithmetic can still solve problems with algebraic reasoning. Sometimes pre-requisite knowledge is essential, but other times, teachers can find creative ways for students to engage with grade-level concepts.

The balance beam problem in Figure 3.3 is an example of accessible algebraic reasoning. Students can see the relationships that keep each beam balanced with equal weights on each side. Students can reason through guidelines for

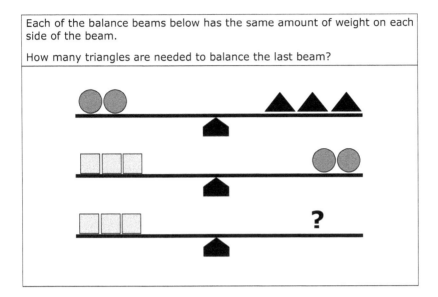

Each of the balance beams below has the same amount of weight on each side of the beam.

How many triangles are needed to balance the last beam?

Figure 3.3 This balance beam problem can be solved by substituting equivalent values on different beams. Students can engage in this algebraic reasoning even if they still struggle with arithmetic skills.

manipulating equations: the beam will continue to balance if the same weights are added or removed from each side, for example.

Students do not need to know arithmetic to engage in the algebraic thinking necessary to solve the balance beam problem. Students who have not memorized their multiplication tables can still solve the algebra problem represented in this figure. While teachers continue to help students fill in prior learning gaps, they can also identify areas of student readiness where students can access the same content as their grade-level peers. This may require scaffolds or creative strategies, but it is usually preferable for students to work on grade-appropriate tasks instead of prior-year learning gaps whenever possible.

References

Martin, C. (2020). Accelerating unfinished learning. *Mathematics Teacher: Learning and Teaching PK-12, 113*(10), 774–776.

Paige, D. D., Sizemore, J. M., & Neace, W. P. (2013). Working inside the box. *NASSP Bulletin, 97*(2), 105–123. 10.1177/0192636512473505

Vygotsky, L. S. (1978). *Mind in society: The development of higher mental processes.* Harvard University Press.

4   Crafting Learning Targets

In my first years of teaching, one of my primary concerns was filling the class time. I would sometimes rehearse direct instruction to predict how long it would take. It was important to me that students were *doing* something for the entire class period, and I often had additional tasks prepared to keep students busy if necessary. My concern was filling the time and I would design or select assignments based on how well they filled those minutes. It was a key component of my behavior management strategy, believing busy students would not have time to break class rules. I also felt that if students were *doing math,* it somehow meant they were learning.

Years later, as I worked within a professional learning community (PLC), we had clearly established learner outcomes. We had predetermined what students should be learning and how students could demonstrate that learning. My perspective switched. I was no longer choosing classroom tasks based on how well they filled the time, but rather I chose classwork that would help students master the priority skills our PLC had identified. If my students needed to be able to explain what a point on a coordinate graph represents in a real-world context, I looked for the most appropriate activities to help students develop and demonstrate that skill.

As I coach teachers, I have observed this same change in perspective as young teachers gain experience and comfort in their roles. Initially, new teachers are often most interested in what students will *do* in class tomorrow. They ask for concrete resources, such as textbooks or worksheets that are filled with *things* for students to *do.* Later in their careers, most teachers begin thinking about what students should *know* and *how* they should learn it. This shifts the focus from concrete things like books and worksheets to more abstract resources, like what questions teachers will ask or what conversations students should engage in.

Filling a class period with meaningful, content-relevant tasks is important. When a teacher returns from a day off campus, they may hope the substitute teacher was able to keep students occupied and out of trouble, but it is not the ultimate measure of an effective classroom. Rather we look for evidence that students are developing new skills and progressing toward curricular goals.

DOI: 10.4324/9781003346333-7

Well-crafted learning targets are the roadmap to direct student learning. Creating learning targets is a vital step in planning instruction. Clear learning targets serve several purposes in the secondary math classroom. Effective learning goals will:

- Guide teachers by indicating what skills and knowledge students should learn.
- Establish benchmarks teachers can use to determine when students have met their learning goals.
- Engage students by communicating goals to self-monitor their own academic progress.

There are many different approaches to crafting learning targets, and this chapter will provide some resources for math teachers to use as they plan.

Breaking Down Math Standards

Curriculum documents often contain broad descriptions of student skills. An Algebra standard might include a long list of skills, asking students to solve quadratic equations in real-world and mathematical contexts by factoring, graphing, or applying the quadratic formula. That one standard includes several weeks' worth of instruction, and it is helpful for teachers to identify the individual components of that math standard. By breaking standards down into small chunks, teachers will find it easier to plan daily instruction, identify and address students' knowledge gaps, and monitor students' progress. Teachers can assess what specific skills students have now and better decide what skills students are ready to develop next.

A powerful first step in the process of crafting learning targets is breaking down the curriculum standard into its components. Teachers can start by literally splitting the standard into a list of separate statements. It is important to identify what students are expected to do (e.g. factor a quadratic function, graph a quadratic function on a coordinate plane, or apply the quadratic formula) and identify the context in which students will work (e.g. from a real-world problem, given a table of values, or using technology). As the example in Table 4.1 illustrates, at this stage, teachers are simply rewriting the original standard into a series of separate statements.

As Table 4.1 shows, a single curriculum standard can contain many skills. The next step is to write learning targets by grouping these skills into manageable chunks. Often these chunks will represent a day or two of instruction. Teachers may have some choices to make depending on students' skills and interests. In the example from Table 4.1, teachers may choose to group these skills based on what information students are given. In that case, the learning targets to cover this curriculum standard may look like this:

- The student will identify the slope and y-intercept of a real-world or mathematical linear relationship from a graph.

Table 4.1 A single curriculum standard is broken down into component skills and contexts

---

Original curriculum standard:
The learner will identify the slope and y-intercept of linear relationships from tables, graphs, equations, and verbal descriptions arising from real-world or mathematical problems.

Skill:	**Context:**
• Identify the slope from a graph	From a mathematical problem
• Identify the slope from a table	
• Identify the slope from an equation	
• Identify the slope from a description	
• Identify the y-intercept from a graph	
• Identify the y-intercept from a table	
• Identify the y-intercept from an equation	
• Identify the y-intercept from a description	

Skill:	**Context:**
• Identify the slope from a graph	From a real-world situation
• Identify the slope from a table	
• Identify the slope from an equation	
• Identify the slope from a description	
• Identify the y-intercept from a graph	
• Identify the y-intercept from a table	
• Identify the y-intercept from an equation	
• Identify the y-intercept from a description	

- The student will identify the slope and y-intercept of a real-world or mathematical linear relationship from a table.
- The student will identify the slope and y-intercept of a real-world or mathematical linear relationship from an equation.
- The student will identify the slope and y-intercept of a real-world or mathematical linear relationship from a verbal description.

Alternatively, teachers may organize this instruction by focusing on what information students are deriving. That sequence of learning targets may look like this:

- The student will identify the slope of a real-world or mathematical linear relationship from a graph or table.
- The student will identify the slope of a real-world or mathematical linear relationship from an equation or verbal description.
- The student will identify the y-intercept of a real-world or mathematical linear relationship from a graph or table.
- The student will identify the y-intercept of a real-world or mathematical linear relationship from an equation or verbal description.

Notice in this list, some information sources were grouped. The first learning target asks students to identify the slope given a graph *or* a table. This could be broken into two separate learning targets if teachers believe students will need more time for each skill. Teachers should find a balance between broad learning targets that include too many skills to precisely assess and overly narrow targets that detract from the natural flow of the curriculum.

Once teachers have a clearer view of the components of a single standard, it is helpful to list what prior knowledge and skills students will use to employ. For example, if an 8th-grade student is expected to create a trend line to represent a set of data, this may require the student to plot points in the first quadrant of the coordinate plane and identify independent and dependent variables. Table 4.2 displays a sample list of prior knowledge skills related to calculating the slope and y-intercept of a linear relationship.

Generating the list of prerequisite skills helps teachers anticipate where students may struggle. In some cases, teachers may be able to build on student strengths and help students solve problems with an alternate approach. For example, if a student has difficulty identifying the slope and y-intercept from a table, they may be able to plot the points from the table and identify the slope and y-intercept from the resulting graph.

Other times, teachers may be able to accommodate the task by inserting scaffolds that allow the student to successfully engage with the problem. Struggling students may be able to identify the slope and the y-intercept from a table as long as the independent values are consecutive numbers beginning with 0: 0, 1, 2, 3, 4, ... If this is the case, teachers can teach students how to rewrite any table in this format and calculate any necessary values to fill in these rows of the table.

Identifying both on-level and prior grade-level pre-requisite skills, as shown in Table 4.2, will help teachers find resources in the vertical alignment to fill

Table 4.2 Distinguishing prior knowledge from the current grade level and prior grade levels can help teachers recognize how to assess students' readiness and help prioritize which skills to emphasize when filling gaps

Original curriculum standard:
The learner will identify the slope and y-intercept of linear relationships from tables, graphs, equations, and verbal descriptions arising from real-world or mathematical problems.

On Grade Level Prior Knowledge:	**Prior Grade Level Skills:**
• Rewrite equations in slope-intercept form	• Locate points on the coordinate plane
• Understand the meaning of the y-intercept in a real-world context	• Calculate the difference between values in a table
• Use the change in independent and dependent values to calculate the slope	• Read the axes on a graph
	• Describe the rate of change in terms of real-world context

in knowledge gaps that some students may exhibit. This approach allows students to access grade-level content even with missing gaps in prior knowledge. Often math students – even those without IEPs – have not yet mastered prerequisite skills from prior grades. While teachers may need to address many of those prior skills (either through quick reviews or more intensive reteaches), teachers do not need to address all of a student's learning gaps before engaging in the current grade-level work. Rather, teachers can identify the specific skills students need for the current learning target and focus on developing students' knowledge and skills in those specific areas (Martin, 2020). There are many topics in algebra and geometry that students can explore even while still mastering content from the middle school curriculum. When teachers are specific in what prior knowledge and skills students need for the current work, they can streamline the process of allowing students to engage in as much grade-level math as possible.

Defining Mastery

Writing a learning target helps teachers and students understand what learning should take place, but it can be difficult to write a concise learning target that is student-friendly while also completely describing a teacher's expectations. A learning target like, "The student will order rational numbers on a number line" is concise, but three different teachers might still interpret this very differently. Should this learning target include negative values? Will students order numbers expressed in scientific notation? Will fractions and decimals be mixed in the same task? It is important for teachers to define what mastery of a learning target will look like. They should decide what level of rigor they are looking for in students' work. This is a question that many professional learning communities explore as teachers reach a consensus definition of student mastery.

One concrete way to define mastery of a learning target is to create a list of mastery questions students should be able to address during their learning. These are questions that teachers might ask as they work with students or students might use in peer discussions. For a learning target that states, "Students will use the Pythagorean Theorem to determine if a triangle contains a right angle," teachers' mastery questions might include:

- How are the three sides of a right triangle related?
- How is the relationship between the sides of a triangle different if the triangle is not a right triangle?
- What information would we have to use to test for a right angle using the Pythagorean Theorem?

These questions can guide the design of instruction. Teachers should consider what learning experiences will help students discover the answers to these questions. For example, to help students contrast the relationship between the sides of right triangles and non-right triangles, teachers might ask students to evaluate the Pythagorean equation for several different triangles and observe the results.

Mastery questions can also guide the pace of classroom instruction. Students each learn at their own pace, and that means some students will master a concept before they have reached the end of their assignment. Other students may take multiple diverse assignments to grasp the underlying concept. This may not happen at the pace that the bell schedule or pacing calendar anticipated. The purpose of math class is not to complete a certain amount of activities, worksheets, problems, or calculations. The purpose is student learning. The mastery questions will indicate to a teacher when a student is ready to move on to new learning. If a student is halfway through a task and can confidently answer the mastery questions, further practice may bore them and reduce engagement. If another student has completed the task and is still unable to discuss the mastery questions, the teacher needs to reevaluate the instruction and usually proceed with a new task that addresses the skill from a different perspective.

I once visited a small classroom of four students with IEPs who each struggled in math. The students were seated at a table with their teacher working through an activity related to one-variable inequalities. The goal of the day's lesson was to give students practice evaluating an inequality to see if a given value was a solution. Students were instructed to roll a die, substitute the number they rolled into a given inequality, then determine if that value made the inequality true or false.

I could tell that students were not moving through this activity as quickly as the teacher anticipated. One student was not able to subitize, so determining the number she rolled on her die was a challenge. Another student had trouble entering negative values into their four-function calculator. As time went on, the teacher became more and more anxious for students to complete this assignment before the end of class. She began suggesting a variety of shortcuts so students could finish on time. As one student rolled his die, the teacher would pick up a pencil and rewrite the inequalities on his paper, substituting the number he rolled for the variables in the inequality. The teacher kept correcting the student who could not subitize when she miscounted the pips on her die, "No, you got it wrong. Count them again."

In the last few minutes before the bell rang to dismiss class, the teacher even filled in a couple of answers on one student's paper so she could feel the assignments had been *completed* before the end of class.

This scene was disheartening. The teacher was focused on completing the task regardless of what learning was (or wasn't) happening. Instead of emphasizing the meaning of each inequality symbol, the process of substitution, or evaluating expressions, the teacher had twisted this task to focus on counting pips on a die and performing arithmetic quickly. Each time the teacher recommended a shortcut to her students, the task moved further away from its intended learning goals. The teacher and students were merely going through the actions and *checking a box* by completing a task without accomplishing any real learning.

If the teacher had kept a list of mastery questions in mind, it might have focused her work with the students. It is true that using dice introduced an engaging way to randomize the task, but it added to the struggle of the student who could not count the dots on the face of her die. If the teacher had used mastery questions to guide her work, she might have replaced that aspect of the task with something that kept the focus on substitution and testing inequalities (perhaps simply giving the student a list of numbers or a die with printed numerals instead of dots). Implementing mastery questions helps teachers keep their focus on essential learning. They remind teachers what points to emphasize as students are working and help teachers gauge when essential learning has happened.

Another strategy to define mastery is to create or select sample math problems that represent what students should be able to solve. This gives both teachers and students a very concrete description of what students should be able to do when they have mastered the learning target. Teachers can use this set of exemplar problems to monitor students' progress and as a guide when creating assessments. These exemplars should communicate the level of rigor that is expected of students. Teachers can share exemplar problems with students at the beginning of the instruction to help students understand the purpose of their current learning. This gives students direction, knowing they have mastered a concept when they can confidently work the exemplar problems.

Guiding Instructional Design

Learning targets, mastery questions, and exemplar problems should guide instruction. That means teachers will normally craft these elements before designing instruction. As teachers locate or create lessons and classroom activities, they should compare those activities against the learning targets and other guiding elements. Teachers have to fight a constant temptation to choose activities based on mediocre criteria: it fits neatly within the time frame, it included a fun theme that will engage students, it was a convenient activity that has already been created, and many others. However, when teachers use learning targets as the ultimate criteria for lesson design, it can lead to several benefits in the classroom:

- Directing reteach for struggling learners – Ideally, teachers (and students) know exactly what learning targets are tied to each classroom assignment. If a student struggles with that assignment or missed an assignment due to an absence, the teacher has a strong indication of what skills to address with the student. Any makeup work or reteach activity can be tailored to the student's needs. For students with IEPs and struggling learners, this means teachers can efficiently focus on areas they need to address.

- Connecting lessons together into a coherent curriculum – Since teachers craft their learning targets prior to designing instruction, they usually see the scope of several weeks' worth of instruction. This allows teachers to write learning targets that build off of each other and arrange them in a meaningful way. When instruction is then aligned to these targets, the students will experience a logical learning sequence which can in turn benefit students with retention issues or attention deficit concerns.
- Better aligned assessments – Clear learning targets provide a guide for both classroom instruction and assessment. When both are aligned to the learning targets, they will also be aligned with each other. This approach means tests will provide a clearer picture of student learning because tests will cover exactly the goals that were addressed during instruction. This provides better data for IEP goals and ARD reviews.
- Student progress monitoring – Students can more easily monitor their own learning progress when classroom assignments are directly linked to learning targets. Students know exactly what skill they should demonstrate with each task, so their performance on the task indicates their level of mastery of the matching learning target. This can increase learner engagement as they observe the progress they are making toward instructional goals.
- More efficient instruction – Aligning instruction with clear learning targets means that students and teachers are spending their time and energy on the content that matters most. Students will not expend class time with unaligned tasks, but rather they can focus on the relevant content for the current course.

Teachers are pulled in many directions, and it is an insurmountable challenge to adequately address a year's worth of math content in one school year – disregarding learning gaps and necessary review. Clear learning targets, mastery questions, and exemplar problems will help teachers maximize their classroom time to help students reach as many of the year's instructional goals as possible.

Reference

Martin, C. (2020). Accelerating unfinished learning. *Mathematics Teacher: Learning and Teaching PK-12, 113*(10), 774–776.

5 Planning Differentiation

Even with well-crafted learning targets, it takes careful planning to effectively reach all of the students in a classroom. Each learner works at their own pace, brings their own prior knowledge and unique perspective, and makes meaning in their own way. As we plan, we also look for opportunities to differentiate the lesson. How can we make sure that all students are able to access the task and reach the learning goals? Sometimes that means changing the timeline so some students can continue working after others have achieved mastery. In some cases we provide support, so more students can effectively engage in the math needed to complete the task. At times, we may even introduce alternate learning targets so that each student can make progress toward an achievable and meaningful goal.

When we differentiate a lesson, we acknowledge that not all students will reach the learning targets at the same pace and along the same pathways. We need to build instruction that is flexible enough to meet the needs, interests, and abilities of the diverse community of students in our classrooms. When we attempt to shepherd all of our students through the same task in the same amount of time, we limit the opportunities for learning and usually create unnecessary frustration.

Anticipating Challenges

When we design our learning targets, we often begin noticing specific areas where students are likely to encounter challenges. Table 5.1 shows an example of a middle school learning target and some opportunities for differentiation. Following the learning target, the table lists some of the prior knowledge and skills students will need and aspects of the learning target where we anticipate some students will need additional support.

This list of prior knowledge and potential obstacles is vital to planning differentiation. This is how we develop a clear picture of how students will develop a new skill. If we overlook this step, we may underestimate the difficulty of the learning goal and soon find that our pacing calendars are unreasonable.

DOI: 10.4324/9781003346333-8

Table 5.1 By analyzing a learning target in this manner, teachers can prepare for challenges students might face

---

Learning Target:

Students will graph the solution of a one-variable inequality on a number line.

Prior Knowledge

- Locating positive and negative numbers on a number line.
- Applying inverse operations to simplify an equation.
- Verifying whether a given value is a solution to an equation.

Potential Obstacles

- Determining whether to use an open or closed circle to represent the inflection point on the number line.
- Distinguishing inequality symbols and their meanings.
- Understanding the effect of inverse operations on the inequality relationship.

Draw point *A* on the number line at -2.5.
Draw point *B* on the number line at 2¾.

Figure 5.1 Short tasks like this example can provide valuable information about students' mastery of prior knowledge.

Once we have listed the prior knowledge and skills that students will use in our class, we can plan pre-assessments to inform our lesson planning. In the list above, we noted that students will use the prior skill of "locating positive and negative numbers on a number line." With a short, five-minute exit ticket, like the example in Figure 5.1, we can learn about our students' current abilities in this area.

The problem in Figure 5.1 can provide a quick snapshot of each student's ability to place numbers on a number line. With a quick scan of these papers, a teacher can see which students need a review of number lines before learning more about inequalities.

The list of potential obstacles helps us anticipate what to look for in student work to make sure they are mastering the skills they need. If we expect, for example, that students may be confused about when to use open or closed circles to represent an inequality, we will build instruction and practice to emphasize that knowledge. When we work with students, we will ask questions specifically about that aspect:

- "I see you shaded in this circle; can you explain why?"
- "What would I have to change in the problem if I wanted you to draw an open circle?"

We expect some students may need interventions or short reteaches over some of these potential obstacles, and we can plan for that in advance.

Creating the list of prior skills and potential obstacles can be particularly challenging for teachers who are teaching their content or grade level for the first time. Whenever possible, it is helpful to draw on the experience of other teachers for insight into how students learn. One of the most helpful practices, however, is working out practice questions *using the same skills your students would.* If your students would calculate by hand, then put away the calculator. If your students struggle with simplifying fractions, then multiply and divide fractions without simplifying them first. Work the problem out with the math skills your students bring to the table so you can understand what they will experience during your assignment.

In Figure 5.2 we see two approaches to a multiplication problem that a typical middle school student might use. Working the problem with the skills of a middle school student highlights the challenge they will experience. Our students may not have the number fluency to quickly recognize that half of the four-fifths will be two-fifths, so their solution strategies will be much more involved. By working out the problem, we recognize that an expression that we might quickly evaluate in passing will take significant time and reasoning from our students.

Working through tasks and sample problems in this manner helps us anticipate where students need support. Then we can use that knowledge to design differentiation into our class work. Particularly for teachers who are new to the content, this strategy is an efficient way to design more accessible work. It is always beneficial to completely work out tasks and problems that we assign to our students, but even in the early stages of our planning, we can learn about how our students will develop a skill or concept by working out sample problems.

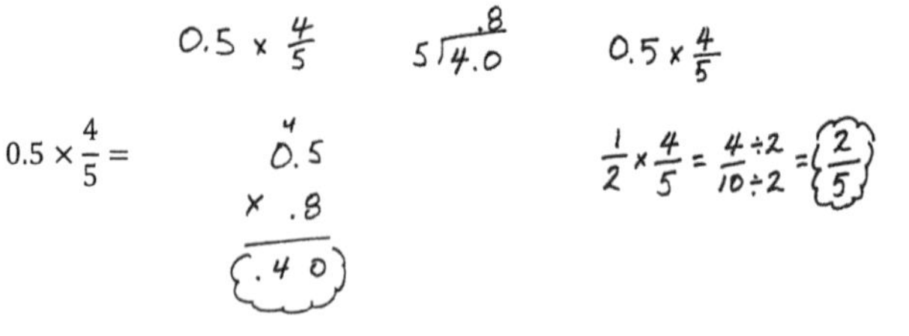

Figure 5.2 There are multiple approaches typical middle school students might use to solve this problem. Anticipating student solutions helps teachers prepare to provide support when necessary.

Table 5.2 Each assessment problem can have a lengthy list of prerequisite knowledge and skills

---

Assessment Problem:

Dylan is planting a flowerbed in the shape of a circle. The flowerbed measures 12 feet across. What is the area of the flowerbed?

Necessary Knowledge and Skills:

- Identify parts of a circle (circumference, diameter, radius)
- Calculate the radius of a circle, given the diameter
- Identify the formula for the area of a circle
- Substitute and evaluate a formula (including the use of exponents)
- Identify the value of π
- Multiply by a decimal

If you or your team of teachers write assessments before planning a unit, work through the assessment problems from a student perspective. As you work through these problems, maintain a list of the skills students need. Table 5.2 shows an example of the list of knowledge and skills students might use to solve a question about the area of a circle.

Next, we can review this list of skills and consider whether they should be essential to this concept. In the example above, we see that in order to determine the area of a circle, students will also need to be familiar with exponents and multiplying by decimals. These are areas where we may need to design differentiation to meet the needs of our students. For students with IEPs, we want to build on their strengths, allowing them to perform meaningful math without obstacles. We should be aware of the challenges facing students with lower processing speed. The list of knowledge and skills above suggests that some students may spend so much time processing tangential skills like multiplication or deciphering exponents and miss out on the more relevant ideas of identifying the parts of a circle or applying the meaning of area. We can address this by providing students with calculation aids or asking students to write an expression for the area of the flowerbed without actually evaluating the expression.

Differentiating instruction does not mean that we need to deny some students access to meaningful math instruction. We are not removing the rich math from our lessons, we are identifying ways for all students to access that rich math. One of our chief strategies will be choosing mathematical tasks that are flexible, open-ended, and leave plenty of room for student thinking.

Flexible Tasks

One year, as my co-teacher and I discussed an upcoming series of lessons on unit rates and proportional reasoning, my co-teacher's creative nature took over and we began constructing a collection of tasks that directly supported our learning objectives and were filled with real-world context.

At the beginning of Monday's class, my co-teacher started weaving a tall tale. He told the class that he and I had been at the big box store down the street from the school when we noticed the manager working late changing signs on the shelves. We told our students that a recent labor shortage had left the manager scrambling to update the store's price tags that displayed the item's cost and its unit price.

We (allegedly) told the manager our students were experts in that sort of thing and invited our classes to audition for a chance to help out an exhausted manager. With that, we launched into a task where students worked in groups, checking each other's reasoning, as they created sample price tags for several items.

Over the next several days, we collected work from our students and brought back more information and requests from our imaginary store manager (Figure 5.3). She wondered if the students could help shoppers use unit prices to identify which item was the best buy. Would the students be willing to help her determine a fair price for some new bulk items the store was carrying?.

Each task allowed students to apply the math they were learning, and it also gave us opportunities to formatively assess their reasoning. We could pull small groups of students who needed some coaching. We encouraged students to share their thinking with classmates and listen to each other's different approaches to the same assignment. We could also subtly adjust most of the tasks to accommodate different learners. We found that we did not need to

Figure 5.3 This is an example price tag that includes the item's price and its unit price. Beneath the example is a task asking students to complete a price tag by filling in the unit price.

create several versions of each day's task, but we could often change the instructions or vary the length in ways that allowed all students to successfully engage in the work.

This series of tasks lent itself to several different types of differentiation with only minor adjustments on our parts as teachers. We did not have to create entirely new tasks in order for all students to engage in this exploration.

- Students who struggled with verbal reasoning were able to focus on the images of groceries to help them determine the unit rate. We helped students use visual representations and tables to identify equivalent rates.
- Students with a calculation disability due to limited working memory were encouraged to solve problems that avoided extensive decimal division. Calculation aids such as number charts and calculators were available as needed.
- Students who needed additional processing time were allowed to work at their own pace. We did not emphasize the number of problems students completed, but rather the demonstration of understanding.

In fact, allowing students to work at their own pace allowed us the flexibility we needed to make this task successful. After we described the purpose of the price tags to display a unit price and provided students with some samples, we allowed them time to explore the problem in small groups. Then my co-teacher and I could visit with groups of students answering questions and offering advice. Students were engaged in meaningful math, but they were free to use their own approaches at their own speed. Some of them made mistakes and started again, but they were making meaning of the mathematics for themselves.

This activity stands in stark contrast to a textbook page packed with a list of similar problems. Many of our students were used to experiencing a lesson cycle following the *I do, We do, You do* structure. This structure often limits students as the teacher first demonstrates a model problem exactly like the ones students will solve on their own. Next, the class works together at the same pace solving similar problems in what is sometimes described as *guided practice*. Finally, students are liberated to complete more problems, closely mimicking the samples, but finally working independently. This instructional approach perceives the teacher as the source of mathematical knowledge in the classroom. It creates the message that students cannot be trusted to engage in new math that they have been guided through before. This process trains students to replicate procedures they have seen someone else perform, but it does not prepare them to solve new problems or apply their knowledge in new ways. We often hear teachers complain that students are "helpless" or want everything "spoon-fed to them." This is the behavior encouraged by the *I do, We do, You do* structure. Students are expected to wait until they have been trained in the precise steps they should follow for a very specific type of math problem.

Students do not all learn at the same speed, and their learning does not always follow the same path. This is true in any classroom, but more so in a neurodiverse class. Each student brings their own unique perspective, background knowledge, strengths, learning gaps, and interests. Teachers create an incredible challenge when they try to guide all students through the same lesson at the same speed. Inevitably, some students will be bored because the content is below their level or moving too slowly while others will be frustrated by the content they aren't ready for and topics they want time to explore more deeply.

We found much greater success by acknowledging the knowledge and skills our students already possess. As our students explore rich math problems, we can come alongside and add to their growing knowledge, suggest ways they can become more efficient, ask questions to help them make new connections, or recommend approaches that will unlock new avenues of exploration.

Planning for Differentiation

One of the most direct ways to adjust a task for student needs is by allowing students to decide how long they need to work on a task. Some students will master a concept quickly and we should allow them to explore the topic more deeply. Others will take more time, and whenever possible, we want to allow students the time they need. Obviously, the challenge in the classroom is that each student is working at a slightly different pace, and teachers need to manage this diverse class and adhere to some form of pacing calendar.

In these instances, it is important to prioritize what skills students *must* practice and which skills are just *nice* to practice. The pacing calendar may not allow us to give students more time, but we can focus the time we have on the most vital concepts. Often, we can streamline a task, removing the extra pieces so that students can complete their work in less time. Figure 5.4 shows a task intended to help students develop their skills in calculating the area of a triangle. We can see the original version of the task, an alternate task that can be completed in less time, and a third version that allows students to explore more deeply if they have the opportunity.

If the goal of this task is to practice calculating the area of a triangle, the first version incorporates the additional skills of decimal and fraction operations which may challenge some students. The second version allows students to choose the level of challenge with which they are comfortable. By asking students to choose from a list of numbers, we can make sure they do not create a trivial problem, like a triangle with a height of 2 and a width of 2. The third version is more open-ended and allows students some exploration. There are other ways to adjust that question, like asking students to create the largest or smallest triangle possible under certain conditions.

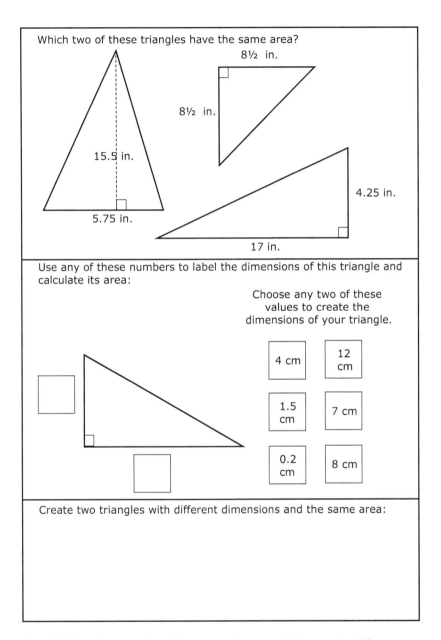

Which two of these triangles have the same area?

8½ in.

8½ in.

15.5 in.

5.75 in.

4.25 in.

17 in.

Use any of these numbers to label the dimensions of this triangle and calculate its area:

Choose any two of these values to create the dimensions of your triangle.

4 cm	12 cm
1.5 cm	7 cm
0.2 cm	8 cm

Create two triangles with different dimensions and the same area:

Figure 5.4 Teachers can adapt tasks to cover the same topic but require different amounts of time to complete.

Each of these examples allows students to practice working with triangles and allows teachers to measure each student's current level of mastery. The adjustments in the task, however, give us a way to differentiate the task to accommodate students who work at different speeds.

Author and researcher Carol Ann Tomlinson (2005) suggests three motives for differentiation: adapting to meet a student's interest, academic readiness, or learner profile. When we offer options that connect with student interest, it can increase engagement and help students connect with the material. The last two reasons, academic readiness and learner profile, are particularly relevant when working with neurodiverse learners.

Academic Readiness refers to the prior knowledge and skills that a student can draw from to work through their current task. In some cases, we may need to adjust learning targets for particular students if the learning gaps are significant enough. We may need to review the concept of area before a student can explore surface area by designing labels for soup cans. Other times, however, we can find alternate pathways for students to access the task. Students who are weak in multiplication facts can still determine the area of shapes by counting the number of squares needed to fill the shape. In fact, this is the approach commonly used to develop the concept of multiplication.

Pre-assessments and student work samples are valuable resources in determining what new learning students are ready for. The student work samples shown in Figure 5.5 were adapted from an activity about butterfly migration. Students created a table to show the relationship between the number of days a butterfly had migrated and the number of miles it had traveled. Examine each student sample taking note of what math students have mastered and what they are ready to learn next.

Student 1's work is typical for middle school students beginning to learn about linear relationships. There are several strengths in the student's work. They have chosen logical input values and correctly calculated the output values. The process column suggests that they recognized the constant rate of change in this relationship: each additional day means the butterfly has traveled an additional 51 miles. Consider what this student is ready to do next: we can discuss the difference between additive relationships and multiplicative relationships. We can try to describe the process in this table using multiplication instead of addition to see if there is more consistency in the expressions we write in the process column.

The next sample from Student 2 shows a student who already recognized the multiplicative relationship in the butterfly's migration. Again, the input values are well-chosen and the output values are calculated correctly. This student wrote expressions in the process column that capture the consistent relationship between the input and output variables. Of course, there is further to go, and this student's teacher should decide what they are ready to do next. We might notice that this student has left the process column blank on the top row next to the input value of zero. We can explore using the same pattern of expressions and

Student 1

x (days)	Process	y (miles)
0	0 + 0 =	0
1	0 + 51 =	51
2	51 + 51 =	102
3	102 + 51 =	153
4	153 + 51 =	204
5	204 + 51 =	255
6	255 + 51 =	306

Student 2

x (days)	Process	y (miles)
0		0
1	1 × 51	51
2	2 × 51	102
3	3 × 51	154
4	4 × 51	204
5	5 × 51	255
6	6 × 51	306

Student 3

x (days)	Process	y (miles)
0	51 −51 = 0	0 miles
1	102 −51 = 51	51 miles
2	153 −51 = 102	102 miles
3	51 × 3 = 153	153 miles
4	153 + 51 = 204	204 miles
5	204 + 51 = 255	255 miles
6	255 + 51 = 306	306 miles

Figure 5.5 Examining student work truly reveals students' current level of understanding.

multiplying 51 by zero. We could also consider generalizing the expressions in the process column by using a variable to represent the input values.

Finally, we see something very different in Student 3's work. This student has done some great math and correctly determined the output values, but the process column shows something very different. It would be appropriate to talk with this student to learn more about their work, but from what we see here, we might guess that they filled out the output column, then went back and created expressions for the process column. They do not seem to understand the purpose of the process column is to communicate the math we used to determine the output value. We see some strong arithmetic skills in this sample, and this student is ready to practice communicating the math they know.

These examples of student work helped us determine the readiness of each learner. We analyzed their current strengths and suggested ways to add to their current understanding. Student 2 is probably ready to discuss writing one-variable equations to generalize a process. Student 3 is not yet ready for that same task. However, there is still meaningful math each student is ready for.

Learner Profile includes several student characteristics such as their ability to comprehend written or spoken information, social skills, or prior academic experiences. Recognizing these traits in our students, we can design instruction to build on their individual strengths. For example, knowing whether a student is stronger in written comprehension or listening comprehension tells us whether to present instructions verbally or in writing. Students with certain behavioral issues or Autism Spectrum Disorder may experience anxiety working in groups or have difficulty communicating with peers. We may need to design additional support for student discourse or when appropriate give students choice in working individually or in groups.

This is distinct from learning styles. Research does not generally support the idea that students learn better when the material is presented in a preferred manner of visual, auditory, or kinesthetic information. Some instruction is best suited to certain presentations, and in fact, students learn better when they can make connections between the information presented in a variety of ways. However, we should consider specific students' strengths when designing instruction.

Universal Design for Learning

At times, we inadvertently prevent students from engaging in tasks because of gaps in language, vocabulary, prior experiences, or other unintended obstacles. Universal Design for Learning (UDL) is a framework that seeks to analyze instruction by identifying and removing obstacles that unnecessarily limit students' access. It can be compared to a physical building where obstacles such as stairs or narrow hallways keep some visitors from accessing its resources. Changing a building's design to widen hallways or install ramps allows all visitors to enter the building. These features are welcoming to everyone. Similarly, some of our classroom tasks cut off students with distracting information, unfamiliar language, or content that is unaligned with our learning goals. Removing those obstacles allows more students to enjoy the learning that can happen in our classrooms.

In describing UDL for math, Lambert (2021) emphasizes that this process begins in the planning stages of a lesson, not after the lesson is created. We can keep the same learning goals but allow students to explore math using different tools or communicate their understanding in different formats. Something as simple as a text-to-speech device that can read text out loud is an example of adapting a task so more students can engage in a task without changing the learning goal.

Teachers should take time to reflect on learning tasks, considering potential learning obstacles that can be removed. We will notice more of those obstacles once students begin working through a task and we observe their work and listen to their conversations. This process will be unique to the specific tasks and students in the classroom, but drawing from our earlier exploration of cognitive processes, there are some general areas to consider.

Processing Speed: Determine which questions to prioritize so that students who work at a slower pace can still engage in thought-provoking work. Too often, traditional assignments start with repetitive procedural practice, concluding with two or three rich contextual problems at the end of the page. This means that students with slower processing speeds either never reach those rich questions or they must work much longer than their peers. Look for problems that can be cut or moved to the end while still allowing students to demonstrate an understanding of the skills they need.

Auditory or Visual Processing: Changes in the classroom environment can benefit some students with auditory or visual processing challenges. We can change seating to reduce distractions from noisy hallways or windows. Consider the layout of assignments and bulletin boards so that there is adequate white space and graphics are not busy. Whenever possible, provide information in multiple formats such as written directions, video, text-to-speech devices, or infographics. Consider alternate methods for students to submit their work such as a narrated video of their work or an oral interview with the teacher.

Fluid Reasoning: Students who struggle to apply their knowledge and skills in new situations may benefit from seeing the connections between their prior work and new tasks. Encourage discussions between students about the content. Make frequent use of group work and partner work. Display anchor charts with key concepts from the curriculum.

Teachers are likely to develop a set of tools to eliminate obstacles from the curriculum in addition to these brief examples listed here. It is important to begin this process while we are still planning the lesson. As we practice anticipating student needs, we can better prepare to notice when students need extra support, and we can be prepared for those moments. Planning for differentiation allows us to remain true to our original learning goal whenever possible, which still allows all students to achieve success.

References

Lambert, Rachel (2021). The magic is in the margins: UDL math. *Mathematics Teacher: Learning and Teaching PK-12, 114*(9), 660–669. 10.5951/MTLT.2020.0282.

Tomlinson, C. A. (2005). *How to differentiate instruction in mixed-ability classrooms*. Pearson/ Merrill Prentice Hall.

Part III
During Instruction

6   Classroom Structures

It is rare for two teachers to have the same mental model of collaborative co-teaching. It is a relatively recent development in instructional practice, and different states, districts, or classrooms have their own terms, definitions, and expectations. Each pair of co-teachers needs to find their own way within the confines of the legal requirements of their roles and the expectations of their supervisors, but this chapter will provide strategies for navigating some of the common challenges and creating an effective learning environment to support diverse learners within a single classroom.

At its core, collaborative co-teaching pairs a general education teacher and a special education teacher in the same classroom to meet the needs of diverse learners. This structure is designed to allow more students to access the general education curriculum and close achievement gaps between general education students and students with IEPs. Ideally, the two co-teachers partner together, equally sharing responsibility for classroom planning, instruction, behavior management, assessment, and IEP data collection. This system is intended to place diverse students in the most appropriate settings while still providing the services and support they need. Collaborative co-teaching has been in practice since the 1990s, and many teacher preparation programs still do not address co-teaching. This leaves some teachers feeling unprepared for the responsibilities of their roles. Professional collaboration can be challenging in any context, and co-teachers must work together to build a common vision for their classroom. Under the right circumstances, co-teaching can be a rewarding collaboration. Building strong co-teach partnerships begins with clear roles, understanding a few high-impact classroom structures, and intentional planning.

Teacher Roles

Some general education math teachers who are new to co-teaching expect their co-teach partners to be content-area experts. This is not a realistic expectation, and it is also not necessary for the success of a co-teach classroom. Co-teaching is not intended to place a second math teacher in the room or provide a source

DOI: 10.4324/9781003346333-10

Table 6.1 This is an example of how co-teach partners may divide classroom responsibilities. These roles will vary between classrooms according to the teachers' skills and experience and students' needs

Typical General Education responsibilities:	Typical Special Education responsibilities:
• Creating and prioritizing content learning targets.	• Identifying opportunities for SDI.
• Measuring students' content knowledge through assessments.	• Selecting strategies for achieving IEP goals.
• Identifying student skills gaps in the vertical alignment.	• Planning SDI.

Shared or negotiated responsibilities:
• Accommodating or modifying assessments and assignments.
• Collecting data on progress toward IEP goals.
• Delivering SDI (under the supervision of the special educator).
• Delivering content instruction (under the supervision of the math teacher).

for in-class math tutoring. Each member of the co-teach pair has their own role to play based on the expertise they bring to the classroom. The general education math teacher is expected to serve as the content expert. They should take primary responsibility for tasks directly related to math instruction, such as prioritizing learning targets, assessing student progress, and identifying content-based supports (e.g. manipulatives such as integer chips or algebra tiles). The special education teacher is present to support the delivery of specially designed instruction (SDI) related to students' IEP goals. They should take primary responsibility for tasks related to SDI, such as identifying opportunities for SDI and selecting strategies that will help the student meet their IEP goals. Both teachers partner together to interweave math instruction and SDI. Each co-teach partnership is unique because of the teachers' individual skills and interests as well as campus or district expectations. However, Table 6.1 lists some of the typical co-teacher responsibilities.

Though it can certainly be an advantage, it is not necessary for the special educator to be a math content expert, just as the general educator does not necessarily need to be trained in SDI and special education services. The co-teach partners do need to find ways to collaborate on classroom instruction, and each teacher's unique knowledge, experience, and comfort level will impact which classroom tasks they will each be able to perform effectively.

Even when co-teachers do not share extensive training in each other's areas of expertise, they can still effectively work together in class to meet the content and SDI needs of their students. For example:

• The math-content teacher can lead a station where students are learning new material while the special educator at another station either reviews prior learning or models and uses a graphic organizer such as a thinking map to break down a word problem.

- The special educator can lead the class through a short warm-up activity or a problem from yesterday's homework while the math-content teacher works with a small group of students to pre-teach some of the math content for today's lesson.
- As students work in small groups, both teachers can circulate between groups monitoring student progress and providing feedback. Teachers can notify each other if a group needs support from a specific co-teacher.

Co-teaching should be an equal partnership between two professional teachers. Each member of the pair brings unique skills, training, and perspective to the classroom, but they must share common goals and visions. One of the top priorities in a co-teach partnership should be ensuring that each teacher has a meaningful role in the classroom each day. This sends a clear message to the students that each teacher is an equal, vital part of the classroom. Additionally, when each teacher plays a meaningful role in the day-to-day operation of the classroom, they will feel their time and effort is important, and they will prioritize their time in the co-teach class. This also discourages administrators from pulling co-teachers to perform other campus duties such as providing substitute coverage for another class or performing lunch duty.

A co-teach pair can divide up classroom duties according to their individual strengths and interests. Each partner will often play a different role in regular responsibilities like data collection, classroom management, managing supplies, attendance, and direct instruction, but usually, these roles are most effective when they are shared between the co-teachers. Classroom management, for example, should not fall on a single member of the pair. Not only would that arrangement create a challenge when the teacher responsible for discipline is absent, but it would make it difficult for students to perceive both teachers as equal partners in the classroom. Instead of assigning classroom management to a single teacher, both partners should agree on classroom policies so they can consistently facilitate the class together. Classroom management is such a vital part of the classroom culture that discussing the details of classroom management is also an opportunity to establish a common vision. Consider these examples of common classroom management questions that co-teachers must address:

- The beginning of class – Do students start class with a warm-up activity, homework review, a journal entry, or does this vary daily? What do we mean when we say a student is "tardy" to class?
- Supplies – What supplies should students bring to class daily? How do teachers respond when a student does not have the supplies they need?

- Parent contact – When do teachers contact a student's parents or guardians and what information is shared? Who is responsible for parent/guardian contact?
- Behavior norms – How do we teach classroom expectations and what are the consequences when students do not meet those expectations?

Answering these questions establishes classroom practice, and it also reveals what each member of the co-teach pair believes about students and learning. Discussing these issues together will help the teaching partners better understand each other's goals for the classroom and individual personalities. As with many working relationships, it is wise to anticipate potential areas of conflict and discuss them before they arise.

Classroom Structures

Sharing a classroom with a co-teacher opens new possibilities for classroom activities and student engagement. There are a few high-impact classroom structures that maximize the benefit of having two teachers in the classroom. Parallel teaching, alternate teaching, and station teaching create active roles for each co-teacher, provide flexibility, and allow students to receive more individualized attention (Friend, 2019). Each structure is simple enough that co-teachers can dive in and try them out, but this section highlights some of the details that can make these structures even more effective.

Parallel Teaching

Parallel teaching divides the class into two groups that are close to the same size. Each co-teacher leads the instruction with one of the groups simultaneously, and each group receives the same general information. Reasons for parallel teaching might include:

- Each group may receive slightly different instruction based on prior readiness.
- One group may practice using a calculation aid or graphic organizer that students in the other group do not require.
- Reducing the class size so teachers can more effectively monitor student progress during instruction.

As with other classroom structures, it is important for co-teachers to discuss how the parallel teaching groups will be determined. In most cases, teachers should intentionally group students, making sure each group contains students both with and without special education support. If parallel teaching is being used to reduce class size and increase teacher monitoring, it may be appropriate to randomly assign students to each teacher's group, but otherwise, students should be grouped according to need, readiness, or interest.

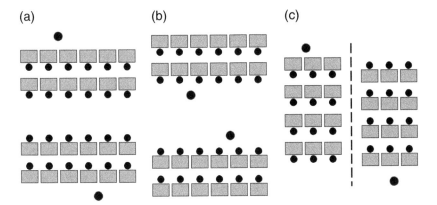

Figure 6.1 (a) Here student desks are positioned so students are facing away from each other, so they won't distract students from the other group. However, teachers are facing each other, so they are projecting their voices directly at each other which can make it difficult for students to focus on a single co-teacher. (b) In this diagram, the co-teachers have positioned themselves behind their students so they can teach and monitor students' work. In this arrangement, teachers are facing away from each other and their voices project only toward their own group. (c) In this arrangement, the student groups are placed side-by-side in a compromise between student distraction and noise levels. In this arrangement, it is helpful to place a physical barrier of whiteboards or desks between the two groups.

One of the primary challenges of parallel teaching is the noise created by two teachers in the same classroom teaching at the same time. Co-teachers should consider this when they arrange the classroom for parallel teaching. One common arrangement places students facing away from each other, with their backs to the other group but places teachers facing each other (Figure 6.1a). In many math classes, this is a common arrangement because it allows teachers to stand in front of their group of students and model math work at the board. Facing student groups away from each other in this manner reduces student distractions, but when teachers face each other, the volume of their instruction can interfere with each other's group. Co-teach partners can develop a signal between themselves when someone needs to lower their voice. Teachers can also position themselves so they are not projecting toward the other group. Some co-teachers stand behind their students as they teach so they can monitor their students' work by looking over their shoulders (Figure 6.1b). This often makes it easier for students to hear just their group's teacher. This arrangement allows the teachers to focus on monitoring student work but moves the teacher away from the board. This is appropriate if the presented material is part of a projected presentation or if students are modeling the work on the board.

If the classroom arrangement permits, an alternate solution is arranging student groups side-by-side (Figure 6.1c). In this arrangement, teachers are not projecting their voices directly at each other, but students are more easily distracted by their peers in the other group. It is helpful to place a physical barrier between the groups. Some co-teach classrooms are equipped with moveable whiteboards or easels that could partition the groups. Even a row of empty desks can reduce distractions between groups.

Alternate Teaching

During alternate teaching, one co-teacher pulls aside a small group of students to work (usually for a short period of time) while the other co-teacher works with the remainder of the class. This can be an opportunity to:

- Review a specific skill with a small group of students (such as a common mistake on a recent test or assignment).
- Pre-teach upcoming content or vocabulary.
- Introduce students to a specific tool or graphic organizer.

It is important to find opportunities for alternate teaching that will not deprive the small group of essential instruction. For example, alternate teaching often happens while the larger section of the class is going over a warm-up activity.

Co-teachers should intentionally select students for the small group. A teacher might work with all the students who missed a particular problem on a recent quiz or all the students who did not finish yesterday's classwork. The small group should be dynamic, changing regularly according to student needs and the topic being addressed. Teachers should not pull the same small group daily, and the small group should not be limited to only students with IEPs. It is important to use this structure regularly in different ways so that students do not attach a stigma to the small group, believing it is used exclusively for struggling students. The small group tasks should also be equally as engaging as the large group task so neither group of students feels punished or rewarded. Imagine the resentment that would form if the large group played an exciting game while the small group copied vocabulary words from a textbook. Perhaps instead, both groups can play modified versions of a similar game, focusing on different skills or streamlining to provide support.

Station Teaching

Station teaching rotates students through several different tasks. A traditional station setup would divide a class into three equal-sized groups that rotate through three stations at regular intervals so that all students visit all stations by the end of the class period. Reasons for station teaching might include:

- Each co-teacher can facilitate a station aligned with their own strengths.
- Students can work through a variety of tasks, such as review, new instruction, and problem-solving strategies.
- Small groups of students can receive tailored instruction according to readiness or need.

Station teaching usually involves at least one task where students work independently. This structure, perhaps more than the others, requires teachers to clearly communicate directions and establish classroom behavior norms.

One fall semester, my co-teacher and I worked with an instructional coach to refine our classroom practice. When our coach asked us if we wanted to work on any particular aspect of the class, we both had the same response: station teaching. My co-teacher and I were struggling to implement stations in our classroom. We divided the class into three groups, established routines for transitioning between stations, and carefully planned activities for each station. We were used to each other's signals so we didn't disturb each other's groups unnecessarily and we could keep our timing on pace. My co-teacher and I each facilitated one station, and the third "independent" station contained a task students could easily complete without our assistance: maybe a vocabulary crossword puzzle, a short video with real-world application of our current content, instructions on organizing their classroom folder, or similar tasks.

The teacher-led stations ran well, but the independent station always seemed like a nightmare. Students working at that station were often out of their seats, wandering around the room, bothering their classmates from other stations, and talking or laughing loudly. My co-teacher and I found we were spending a large portion of our time redirecting behaviors from the independent station instead of leading the tasks for our teacher-led groups.

Our coach suggested that we video-record our classroom to get an objective view of what was happening during our station rotations. So, one day, we propped up a tablet on a desk and started recording. When my co-teacher and I watched the video, of course, we focused on that independent station and the raucous behaviors coming from that corner of the room. We were surprised by what we saw in the video. It wasn't that students were avoiding the work. Most of them entered the station with the best intentions. They picked up their task, read the directions, and started working. Then you could almost see their minds start to wander. The independent task no longer held their attention, and they started looking around the room, noticing friends, finding something distracting out the window, remembering an interesting book in their backpack, anything that was more interesting than a crossword puzzle, a math video, or their classwork folder.

We realized that by trying to make the independent station something that students could do without our assistance, we had lowered the bar and created a busywork station, and the students knew it. Not only was the work boring, but our students knew it didn't really matter. So they found other things to do.

Working with our instructional coach, we changed the types of tasks we assigned at the independent station. We made sure each task required higher-order thinking. Students had to create, analyze, or explain instead of copy and recite. Instead of low-level tasks like a vocabulary crossword puzzle, we used more involved assignments like asking students to create a comic strip using words from a word bank. Passive tasks like watching a video, were replaced with rich writing prompts that asked them to plan a birthday party or design a treehouse to creatively apply the math they were learning.

It did not fix all our problems, but students were much more engaged in the tasks we placed at the independent station. My co-teacher and I were spending less time redirecting independent students and could work with our own stations with fewer interruptions.

This experience highlighted one of the important logistical aspects of station teaching: each station should include a respectful task that is aligned with students' current abilities. If a task is too simple, teachers can increase the rigor by introducing higher-order thinking skills. If a task is too challenging, teachers can provide scaffolds such as graphic organizers, sample problems, or tutorial videos.

Intentional planning for station rotations can also prevent behavioral problems during class. Teachers should consider the profile of individual students when planning for station teaching. IEP goals related to content and behavior will both impact the formation of student groups. Groups do not need to be the same size. Some groups of students can work independently in large groups, while other students are more likely to focus in smaller groups. Be aware of student personalities and relationships when forming groups. Students who struggle with self-discipline should not begin class at an independent station. Rather, they should first work at a teacher-led station to establish classroom expectations before rotating to an independent station later in the class period. Some students may be more productive staying in one location in the classroom near a teacher instead of rotating to different stations.

Station teaching is a very flexible structure, and teachers can create unconventional station setups. For example:

- Students may take several days to rotate through a set of stations. Teachers can leave a set of station tasks arranged in class over a few days. Students may spend part, or all, of each class day working their way through the station activities.
- Different groups of students may complete different tasks. For example, the math content teacher may be leading a station where they teach students to solve proportional reasoning problems using rational scale factors. When one of the groups rotates to this station, however, the teacher switches to

a different task and shows this group how to use a graphic organizer to notice multiplicative relationships within and between the ratios that form a proportion. This arrangement requires careful planning when arranging the student groups.

- Students may rotate independently through stations. Instead of signaling when all students should stop their work and move to the next station, teachers can allow students to work at their own pace and move to another station when they have completed a task.

Station teaching allows for significant differentiation in the classroom. Stations can last for a few minutes or a few days, and the activities can be designed to target a specific group of students.

Suggestions for Planning

Co-teaching often requires more planning and preparation than a traditional classroom. Teachers may need to coordinate the roles they will fill during class, such as who will lead each station. Preparing classroom structures often means pre-arranging student groups and preparing multiple activities. Teachers may need to clarify content or SDI details with their teaching partner. The daily schedule can make planning a challenge, and co-teachers need to maximize the planning opportunities they do have.

First, co-teachers should set realistic expectations for themselves. It is okay to start small, and it is important to continue growing. Co-teachers who are working together for the first time should consider selecting one classroom structure to implement several times until they are comfortable. Once teachers and students have worked out the details, then it is time to branch out to additional structures. Alternate teaching is a good place to start for the new co-teach pairs. It is a high-impact structure with fewer logistical considerations than station teaching, and teachers can plan their group activities independently.

Communication between co-teachers is vital. Both before and during class, teaching partners need to support each other. Some co-teachers can confidently facilitate a station activity with little input from their teaching partner, some are comfortable with only an answer key for any assignments, and others prefer to run through a mock lesson before class. It is important that each teacher can safely ask for whatever level of support they need. Co-teachers who do not have an extensive math content background may want to verify that they are teaching strategies that are mathematically sound. Co-teachers with limited special education training may need to ask if their SDI activity truly addresses an IEP goal. Co-teachers are assigned together because they each bring different areas of expertise. It is important to share that expertise with each other.

During class, co-teachers may need signals to indicate when they are ready to rotate stations. These can be subtle hand signs or a direct inquiry: "How many

more minutes before your group is ready to rotate?" Any teacher who is facil-
itating a station should have a clear picture of what learning students should
accomplish by the end of their time at the station. It is not always important to
finish the task at the station, but there may be some essential demonstration,
practice question, or skill we want students to see before they move on. If some
students have not reached that bar by the time we need to rotate, a teacher can
note that to address during a future alternate teach.

Co-teaching takes many teachers outside of their comfort zone. For decades,
teaching was perceived as a solitary act, and the teacher was the lone authority
in the classroom. This does not reflect the current reality, and effective co-
teaching can benefit students and teachers. As co-teachers become more familiar
with each other and classroom roles, the practices from this chapter become
easier to implement. Developing a common vocabulary around teaching
structures makes communication more effective. Co-teachers will become more
comfortable with their roles and co-teach structures as they find more opportunities to practice and refine them in their own classroom space. Each co-teach
pair – and each student group – is unique, so these structures become most
effective when co-teachers truly make them their own and fit them into their
own classroom goals.

Reference

Friend, M. (2019). *Co-teach!: Building and sustaining effective classroom partnerships in Inclusive
Schools*. Marilyn Friend, Inc.

7 Accommodations and Modifications

Take a moment to read through the math question presented in Figure 7.1.

Imagine you are reviewing class data and you notice that one of your students has chosen answer C: $3x + 5$. Take a moment to list what you know this student understands and what you know this student is still mastering.

You may have struggled to make those lists, and it is likely that another teacher would produce very different lists. This question – and the student's response – leaves ambiguity about the student's current abilities. To correctly answer this question (using traditional methods), a student needs to understand and apply their knowledge of factoring. But students must also know the relationship between the dimensions of a rectangle and its area. Take a moment to also consider the language of the problem. What words are used and what biases do they introduce? Will all of your students understand that a tennis court is shaped like a rectangle? What challenges would an Emergent Bilingual student face when answering this problem? Could a student use alternate approaches to solve this problem that circumvents the target skill of factoring?

Chapter 12 in this book examines assessment more closely, but this sample question – and what it tells us about our students – highlights the need for accommodations and modifications in math class. A typical task or problem in a math class is complicated by the inclusion of content and skills that aren't directly related to math instructional goals (such as vocabulary, contextual information, or test-taking skills). Classroom tasks often weave together several math skills at once, making it difficult to pinpoint which skills a student has mastered and which are still developing. This complexity is an appropriate part of a rich math curriculum, but at times it is necessary to create adjustments for specific students. Consider a student who struggles with fluid reasoning and applying their knowledge and skills to new situations. Our Specially Designed Instruction will likely help this student develop strategies for approaching novel problems, but there will be times we need to directly assess the student's content knowledge without extraneous factors. It may require communication between a general education teacher and a special educator to

DOI: 10.4324/9781003346333-11

The area of a tennis court can be represented with the expression

$$6x^2 + 7x + 2$$

If the width of the tennis court is represented with the expression $3x + 2$, which expression could represent the tennis court's length?

A. $6x^2 + 4x$
B. $2x + 1$
C. $3x + 5$
D. $18x^3 + 33x^2 + 20x + 4$

Figure 7.1 A typical standardized test question.

make sure that accommodations and modifications have the intended result. These adjustments should be tailored to the needs of the specific student and to the specific task and its learning targets. Accommodations and modifications are usually unique to the individual students and are always driven by the student's IEP.

Accommodations and modifications are one way that we allow all students to access a rich math curriculum. We may have students in a classroom with specific learning disabilities in math problem-solving or in math calculation. Typical math tasks (like the sample at the beginning of this chapter) will present different challenges for students with these SLDs. It does not mean students with SLDs cannot participate in the same curriculum as their peers, but it may mean we need to provide alternate routes for them to meaningfully engage in the math content. The goal is to provide exactly the right amount of support to allow students to participate in math class with the appropriate level of productive struggle. If a teacher over-scaffolds and provides too much support, students will not be practicing the skills we intended nor acquiring the math skills we desire. Students are more likely to become bored and act out, or even offended and resentful of over-scaffolding. On the other hand, when teachers do not sufficiently adapt tasks to a student's ability level, students become frustrated and withdraw from the task. This can also lead to behavior problems in the classroom when students recognize that a task is unreasonable or want to divert attention away from their current ability level. Properly adapting a task requires knowledge of:

• The student's current readiness and skillset based on formative assessment.
• The student's strengths and weaknesses as described in the IEP and FIE.
• The task's learning targets and the instructional goal of the assignment.
• The extraneous information embedded in the task such as other math skills or the problem's context.

Adjusting for Student Need

The first consideration is the student's level of readiness. This applies to all students, not just those with IEPs. Consider a unit of study on similar figures and scale factors. Table 7.1 shows a sample learning target and assessment question.

If students have already developed the skill of working with rational numbers, this learning target is an opportunity for spiral review to maintain that skill by practicing it in the context of new math problems. It is appropriate, therefore, for the sample problem above to include decimal dimensions and a scale factor expressed as a mixed number.

It is likely that any math classroom will include some students, however, who are still developing the ability to multiply rational numbers. This deficit will prevent these students from engaging in this assessment question regardless of their knowledge of scale factors and dilations. This sample question will not accurately reveal whether this group of students understands the relationship between a shape, its scale factor, and its dilation because the decimals and mixed numbers in the problem are an obstacle. By replacing the decimal values and mixed numbers in this problem, we can still assess students' knowledge of scale factors and dilation. The adapted question might look like the one shown in Table 7.2.

Notice in this example, the adjustments to the question do not change the learning target. The changes to this question are necessary for students who cannot multiply rational numbers, but in most cases, it would not be appropriate to make this change for all students. If there are students in the classroom who can fluently work with rational numbers, teachers should provide them the

Table 7.1 This is a typical question aligned with a specific learning target

---

Learning Target: The student will use a scale factor to determine the dimensions of a dilated image.

Chris ordered a poster that is an enlargement of a photo he likes. The original photo measures 4.5 inches wide and 3.2 inches tall. The poster will be created using a scale factor of 4½. What will be the dimensions of the poster?

Table 7.2 The adapted version of this question measures the same learning target but removes unrelated skills

---

Learning Target: The student will use a scale factor to determine the dimensions of a dilated image.

Chris ordered a poster that is an enlargement of a photo he likes. The original photo measures 4 inches wide and 3 inches tall. The poster will be created using a scale factor of 6. What will be the dimensions of the poster?

---

opportunity to apply those skills in multiple settings. For some students, the question in Table 7.2 would be over-scaffolded.

Aside from student readiness, for students with IEPs, we should also consider any unique challenges this problem may present. For example, students with an SLD in math problem-solving may be fluent in math calculations but struggle to comprehend how to apply those skills to this problem. During instruction, these students should experience SDI to help them develop and apply strategies to solve problems such as this one. In this case, appropriate SDI might include graphic organizers to help students identify the connections between the pieces of information in the problem. Teachers may help students use highlighting or color coding to prioritize some information from the problem while eliminating distracting details. In addition to the instructional support during this unit, it may be appropriate to scaffold this assessment question as well. The type of adjustments will depend on the specific student and the cause of their SLD in math problem-solving. In addition to providing graphic organizers, the actual question may be adjusted. Some examples are listed in Table 7.3.

For students with an SLD in math calculation, teachers would likely provide some form of calculation aid. Depending on the grade level and the student's fluency, a multiplication chart or calculator may be necessary. If the student's SLD is only in the area of math calculation, the problem may not need further adjustment. Some students, however, will have SLDs in both math calculation and math problem-solving, calling for a combination of approaches.

Accommodations vs. Modifications

Adjusting classroom tasks or assessments requires more than a knowledge of the student's unique strengths and areas of growth. Teachers must also understand the intent of the task and the learning targets it addresses. Whenever possible, teachers should work to create alternate tasks which still address the same learning targets. Sometimes, however, that is not appropriate. This is where accommodations differ from modifications.

An accommodation (Figure 7.2) is an adjustment that makes a task accessible to particular students while still addressing the same learning target. Very basic examples of accommodation would be printing instructions in larger font sizes, translating a task into Braille, or providing a blank graphic organizer. In a math class, this might mean making a graph easier to read, simplifying a table, or changing some of the numerical values in a problem. As long as the task is still addressing the same learning target, the adjustment is an accommodation.

Modifications (Figure 7.3), by contrast, change the learning target. If a student is not yet able to engage with the current learning target, teachers can prepare an alternate task — usually a related learning target in the vertical alignment of the original task. The modified task might remove some layers of complexity or substitute different content. As with accommodations, teachers should design

Table 7.3 Each of these adaptations of the original question is matched to the specific area of student need

---

Student is below average in long-term memory storage and retrieval.

Consider appending a formula to the problem to remind students of the relationship between a figure, its scale factor, and its dilation.

Chris ordered a poster that is an enlargement of a photo he likes. The original photo measures 4.5 inches wide and 3.2 inches tall. The poster will be created using a scale factor of 4½. What will be the dimensions of the poster?

Dilated Dimension = Scale Factor × Original Dimension

Student is below average in fluid reasoning.

Consider removing the context from the problem to focus student's attention on the underlying math.
- A rectangle measures 4.5 inches wide and 3.2 inches tall.
- The rectangle is dilated with a scale factor of 4½. What are the dimensions of the enlargement?

Student is below average in crystallized intelligence.

Consider adding a diagram to the problem showing the original picture with dimensions and the dilation with missing measurements to provide an alternative to verbal information.

Chris ordered a poster that is an enlargement of a photo he likes. The original photo measures 4.5 inches wide and 3.2 inches tall. The poster will be created using a scale factor of 4½.

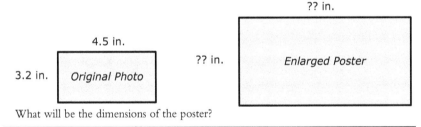

What will be the dimensions of the poster?

---

modifications that represent the least amount of scaffolding necessary for the individual student. Over-scaffolding a modification will impair the student's ability to close learning gaps over time.

Accommodations and modifications are dependent on the circumstances and the learning target. The same adjustment that is an accommodation in one instance, may be a modification in another instance. The question in Figure 7.4, for example, includes a graphic organizer to help students recognize the equivalent ratios in the problem and apply proportional reasoning and their knowledge of multiplication relationships to calculate a missing value.

Original Learning Target: The student will determine the slopes of parallel and perpendicular lines.
A line is graphed on the coordinate plane shown below.

- What is the slope of a line parallel to the graphed line?

- What is the slope of a line perpendicular to the graphed line?

Accommodated Learning Target: The student will determine the slopes of parallel and perpendicular lines.
A line is graphed on the coordinate plane shown below.

- What is the slope of a line parallel to the graphed line?

- What is the slope of a line perpendicular to the graphed line?

$$m = \frac{y_2 - y_1}{x_2 - x_1}$$

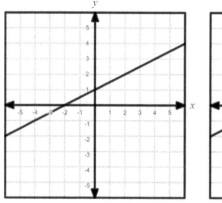
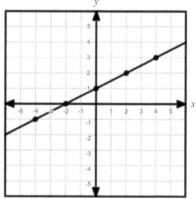

Figure 7.2 The accommodations shown in this example do not change the learning target but help students avoid potential barriers to successfully completing the task.

If the learning target is: "The student will use proportional reasoning to solve problems," this graphic organizer with values from the problem is an accommodation. Students still must identify the multiplicative relationships between the numbers in the table and identify the missing value. However, if the learning target is: "The student will use a proportion to represent real-world situations," then the new version of this question is a modification. Students who work through the adjusted question are not working at the level of rigor described in the learning target. They are working on a separate learning goal, though it is a related skill.

Aside from adjusting tasks and assessment items, there may be other general accommodations for students with SLDs. Providing students with extra time or verbal instructions is very common, but it is important to apply these accommodations only when needed and in accordance with the student's academic profile.

Original Learning Target: The student will determine the area of composite shapes composed of semi-circles, rectangles, and/or triangles.	Modified Learning Target: The student will determine the area of composite shapes composed of ~~semi-circles~~, rectangles, and/or triangles.	Modified Learning Target: The student will determine the area of rectangles and/or triangles.
Determine the area of the shaded region.	Determine the area of the shaded region.	Determine the area of each figure.

Figure 7.3 Each example of a modified question changes the learning target. The modified question may test a subset of the original skills or assess another skill within the vertical alignment of the original task.

The manager at a t-shirt shop notices they sell about 12 t-shirts for every 4 customers who visit the shop. If the shop expects 15 customers on Saturday, how many t-shirts do they expect to sell?

customers	4		15
t-shirts	12		??

Figure 7.4 Depending on the learning target, this adaptation may be an accommodation or a modification.

Oral administration of tests or verbal instructions is intended to support learners who struggle with written language. This can be due to challenges with visual processing or language processing in general. However, many students in this category also struggle with auditory processing and listening comprehension. Teachers need to identify students' strengths and leverage them. For some students, oral administration of assessments or verbal instructions for tasks will place them at a disadvantage. In either case, students will often need continued access to the task or problem, particularly in the cases of students with below-average working memory.

Research is inconsistent on the impact of extended time on the performance of students with SLDs. It is clear this accommodation is not appropriate for all students. As with all accommodations and modifications, it can be abused to the detriment of the student. When a student takes an extended amount of time to complete an assessment, they are often missing the learning task their peers are completing. Extended time on class assignments can cause classwork to stack up and result in a student falling behind. In many cases, it may be a better option to shorten the task or test so the student with SLD can complete the adjusted version in the same amount of time that their classmates complete the original version.

Accommodations and modifications are not one-size-fits-all. It is a red flag when all students with IEPs receive the same support. Each student needs a unique set of accommodations and modifications according to their student profile, IEP goals, and instructional learning targets. Typically, there is no accommodation or modification which is appropriate across the board for all students.

Common Math Accommodations & Modifications

General accommodations are common regardless of the content. Adjustments such as increased white space and font size or removing distracting information can be applied in any subject area. There are some accommodations and modifications, however, that are particularly useful for math assignments.

A typical math task will come with a significant amount of written text. This in itself will be an obstacle to some students. Teachers may choose to chunk this text into individual bullet points, simplify language, or include diagrams to help students process the written language. However, math teachers should also be aware that math text does not follow the same patterns that text usually follows in other content areas. Students learn reading strategies to apply in ELAR, Science, or Social Studies courses, but those strategies may work differently with a typical sample of math text.

Most writing passages begin with an introduction that contains the main idea, followed by several pieces of supporting information, then a conclusion. Consider a math word problem, however, such as the problem in Figure 7.5 about a student shopping for dog food.

This problem begins with an introduction that provides context to the problem, but is not particularly important to the task students must accomplish. What follows are several pieces of supporting information. Finally, the main idea – the question students must answer – is revealed at the end. This pattern is almost the reverse of other writing samples that students encounter in the classroom. This traditional setup requires students to try to organize and hold several pieces of information in working memory before they know what they will do with the information or why it is important.

Figure 7.6 shows a simple revision to this problem.

> Alex's family recently got a new dog, and Alex needs to shop for dog food. At the pet store, large bags of dog food cost $12.50 each, and small bags of dog food cost $5.00 each. If Alex has $40, how many large bags of dog food can they purchase?

Figure 7.5 This is a typical math word problem with extensive text to read.

How many large bags of dog food can Alex purchase?

Alex's family recently got a new dog, and Alex needs to shop for dog food. At the pet store, large bags of dog food cost $12.50 each, and small bags of dog food cost $5.00 each. If Alex has $40, how many large bags of dog food can they purchase?

Figure 7.6 Writing the question at the beginning of the problem provides students with guidance as they read the remaining text.

By placing the question at the beginning of the problem, students have a clear guide for organizing the information they will read. They now have a framework to use as they read the situation, helping them determine which information will be useful in solving the problem. Of course, there are other accommodations available as well. Figure 7.7 presents the problem with chunked text.

Finally, Figure 7.8 contains a version of the problem with extraneous information removed.

How many large bags of dog food can Alex purchase?

Alex's family recently got a new dog, and Alex needs to shop for dog food at the pet store.

- Large bags of dog food cost $12.50 each.
- Small bags of dog food cost $5.00 each.
- Alex has $40.

How many large bags of dog food can Alex purchase?

Figure 7.7 Chunking text can break information into more manageable pieces for students to read and comprehend.

How many large bags of dog food can Alex purchase?

Alex is buying dog food.

- Each bag of dog food costs $12.50.
- Alex has $40.

How many bags of dog food can Alex purchase?

Figure 7.8 Removing extraneous information still measures the same learning target while removing barriers to student performance.

Again, the teacher's goal is to match the correct amount of accommodation to the student, based on readiness, areas of strength, and the nature of the task.

Seeing so many different versions of a single question may cause a teacher to wonder if they will need to create several different versions of a task. Depending on the composition of students in the classroom, that is likely. It is rare that each student with an IEP requires a completely individualized version of a task (though that does happen sometimes). Often teachers can streamline accommodations and modifications and meet the needs of several students with only a couple of adjusted versions of an assignment. If this is a classroom assignment (as opposed to an assessment), teachers can deliver accommodations and modifications in person as they work with a student. Accommodating or modifying a task alongside a student can be a means to foster independence (a key component of SDI). A teacher can model for the student how to adjust a task to make it more accessible, such as by chunking information, completing a graphic organizer, or striking out distracting information. The goal is to make the task accessible without over-scaffolding. The task should address the learning target without creating obstacles to the learning. In a co-teach classroom, this process of accommodating or modifying tasks and assignments is a shared responsibility between the general education math teacher and the special educator. In fact, in some cases, the teacher pair may need to collaborate to make sure the adjustments still maintain the same content learning target and address the student's areas of need and IEP goals.

8 Graphic Organizers

Graphic organizers are a common feature in reading classrooms. Students use a variety of tools such as concept maps, timelines, or story webs to help make sense of the written text. Secondary math work often includes written text as well, and these types of organizational aids can aid student comprehension of word problems. Concept maps can help students see how information is connected or timelines can help clarify the action of a situation. This can be especially helpful in math where numbers can be used in many different ways. It is clarifying simply to identify when a number is used as a quantity (such as "Taylor worked for 3 hours") and when a number is used for relation or comparison (such as "Taylor worked 3 times as many hours as Chris worked") (Kelemanik et al., 2016). Graphic organizers encourage students to take the time to analyze the text before tackling the math involved. Additionally, other forms of graphic organizers can help students make sense of mathematical relationships and how they can use the information to answer questions and solve problems.

As shown in Figure 8.1, the same graphic organizers that are common in reading classrooms can be adapted to the type of reading students must do in math class. The concept map in this diagram provides a way for a student to identify and categorize key information. This specific concept map emphasizes the central question, keeping the focus on how information is related to addressing that problem.

Students can create and use specialized graphic organizers to clarify mathematical relationships when solving problems. Figure 8.2 shows how information from a word problem is reorganized into a table to help students compare two proportional groups of data. This type of graphic organizer requires some prior understanding of the mathematical concept and is used as a tool to answer a question or solve a problem.

Students who struggle with long-term storage and retrieval can benefit from graphic organizers which help them recall the knowledge and skills they need to apply to particular types of problems. Graphic organizers can remind them, for example, what information they need to identify in a proportional relationship, the attributes of a quadratic function, or the relationship between the area and perimeter of a polygon.

DOI: 10.4324/9781003346333-12

Maria is going to rent a car for a trip out of town. She is comparing the prices from two companies. Lakeside Rentals charges $40 per day and $0.75 per mile to rent one of their cars. Boardwalk Cars charges $25 per day and $1.50 per miles to rent the same type of car. Maria needs to rent the car for 4 days. How can she determine which company offers her the better deal?

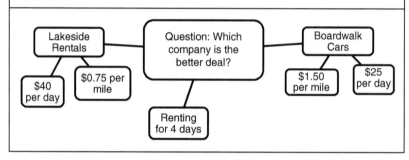

Figure 8.1 This is an example of a concept map used to organize information in a math task that would normally be solved by using a system of equations.

Coach Brown and Coach Mesa both teach high school athletics, and their classes have the same ratio of juniors to seniors. Coach Brown's class has 30 juniors and 24 seniors. Coach Mesa's class has 45 students. How many juniors and how many seniors are in Coach Mesa's class?

	Coach Brown	Coach Mesa
Juniors	30	25
Seniors	24	20
Total	54	45

Figure 8.2 A simple table can be used as a graphic organizer to arrange corresponding pieces of information. In this example, it helps to make the proportional relationships more visible. The clear cells contain information explicitly stated in the problem. The gray-shaded cells contain information that the student had to derive using addition or proportional reasoning.

For students with limited working memory, graphic organizers can provide a place for them to consistently store information so they can find it later. Graphic organizers can allow students to take the information hidden in a word problem and arrange it in a familiar layout.

High-Impact Graphic Organizers

Graphic organizers that address specific math concepts should be simple for students to understand and complete. If the graphic organizer becomes a cumbersome task, students are less likely to use it, or they may become confused about its application. Figure 8.3 shows an example of a graphic organizer that helps students apply the Pythagorean theorem to observe the relationship between the sides of a right triangle.

There are generally six pieces of information students may be provided in a problem that uses the Pythagorean theorem. The triangle has three sides and the Pythagorean theorem connects the squares of those sides. This graphic organizer guides students to identify any of those six pieces of information they have been given and reminds them they can use that information to learn more. Depending on the problem students are trying to solve, they may not need to complete the entire graphic organizer. It is simply a tool to help them identify the information they know and make a plan for finding the information they are looking for. This graphic organizer is simple enough that students can remember how to complete it and they can create it on their own if necessary.

Effective graphic organizers also focus on concepts instead of procedures. Notice the Pythagorean theorem tool in Figure 8.3 focused on the relationship between the sides of a right triangle and the squares of those sides. The graphic organizer did not reduce the Pythagorean theorem to a list of rote steps but rather encouraged students to apply the relationship as necessary.

The tool shown in Figure 8.4 also focuses on geometric relationships. This graphic organizer displays the relationship between the parts of a circle. It includes an image of a circle and a chart representing the relative lengths of the circle's radius, diameter, and circumference.

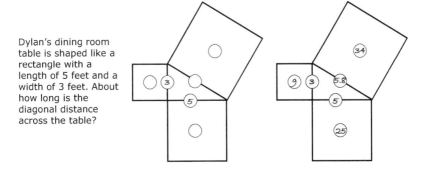

Dylan's dining room table is shaped like a rectangle with a length of 5 feet and a width of 3 feet. About how long is the diagonal distance across the table?

Figure 8.3 This graphic organizer helps students identify and sort the information they may be given in a problem that applies the Pythagorean theorem. Students label the lengths of any of the triangle's sides and the area of any of the adjacent squares (shown in the left diagram). Students can calculate any additional values that may help them answer questions (as shown in the right diagram).

A circular flower garden has a tree planted in the center and is surrounded by a 12-foot long ring of bricks. How far is the distance from the tree to the edge of the flower garden?

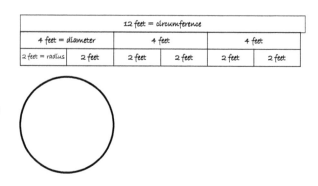

12 feet = circumference					
4 feet = diameter		4 feet		4 feet	
2 feet = radius	2 feet	2 feet	2 feet	2 feet	2 feet

Figure 8.4 This graphic organizer reminds students of the relationship between the radius, diameter, and circumference of a circle. The chart provides an area for students to sort that information and calculate other missing information.

The purpose of the tool is to help students identify what information they already have and then see how they can use that information to learn more. For example, if a student knows the radius of a circle, they see that the diameter is twice the length of the radius. The organization of this information makes it easy for students to work up or down the chart to find any missing information. Again, the focus is on the mathematical relationships (the circumference is equal to about three diameters, and the radius is half of the diameter) and not rote procedures. We aren't directing students to calculate the radius by dividing the diameter by two. Rather we are helping students see that relationship and arrive at a strategy on their own. This will improve retention and increase students' math reasoning skills which they can continue to apply in other settings.

Instruction for Graphic Organizers

During my first several years as a teacher, I believed graphic organizers and other paper-based scaffolds could truly help my students solve the sorts of math problems they encountered in my classroom. I made copies of blank graphic organizers along with other supports such as multiplication charts, and pages of formulas for reference. Then I carefully curated those pages by placing them in neat binders on a shelf. Most years I even made sure my students knew where to find them if they wanted them.

And that's all I did.

Needless to say, my students didn't get many benefits from those binders I spent so much time preparing. I did not teach my students how to use the tools I prepared. I did not create any intentional practice to highlight the role of each support. I did not review their use over an extended period of time so my students would remember what was in the binder and how to use it.

In addition, if one of my students did decide to take advantage of the graphic organizers and reference material in my classroom, they would have been forced to walk across the room and retrieve it from the shelf. They would have announced to the entire class their need for special assistance. I didn't make the tools easily accessible and I inadvertently attached a stigma to their use by implying that most students would never need to use them.

Fortunately, over the years, I changed my practice and started taking the time to teach my students how to use graphic organizers and other resources. I also made sure all students could use the tools they needed without feeling like it meant they were struggling with math.

Teach Students How to Use the Graphic Organizer

First of all, it is important to teach students about the graphic organizer so they understand how to use it to answer questions. This step usually would come after students have some initial knowledge of the concept related to the graphic organizer. Students need enough background knowledge so the tool will make sense and they can see its value in helping to organize information or streamline their work. In Figure 8.5 we see how a simple blank table can be used to help students identify the y-intercept of a linear relationship using data from a table.

This approach would probably be introduced after students have a working knowledge of the y-intercept. We want students to understand that we can recognize the y-intercept in a table of values because it is the point with an x value of zero. In the problem from Figure 8.5, students must determine the y-intercept because this value is not currently part of the table. The choice of points to include in the table can make this problem especially challenging.

The teacher can help students determine the y-intercept using a blank table. Working with the whole class or a small group, the teacher can begin by asking students to describe what the question is asking for and why the problem is challenging. Students should be able to describe the y-intercept and how it can be recognized in a table. They should also be able to explain that the y-intercept is not included in this table.

Next, the teacher can remind students that the table includes only a few of the points that represent this linear relationship. The teacher can suggest that the problem would be much easier with the list of x values shown in Stage 2 of Figure 8.5. Students can be invited to transfer information from the original table into the graphic organizer.

Finally, students can reason the missing values in the table, remembering that this is a linear relationship. Using a constant rate of change, students can determine the y value for the first row of the table (shown in Stage 3 of Figure 8.5) which represents the y-intercept.

In this approach, the teacher first made sure students had the prerequisite knowledge to use the graphic organizer. Next, the teacher helped students leverage

Determine the y - intercept of the linear relationship displayed in the table below.	Determine the y - intercept of the linear relationship displayed in the table below.	Determine the y - intercept of the linear relationship displayed in the table below.

x	y
3	17
5	27
7	37

x	y
3	17
5	27
7	37

x	y
3	17
5	27
7	37

x	y

x	y
0	
1	
2	
3	
4	
5	
6	
7	

x	y
0	
1	
2	
3	17
4	
5	27
6	
7	37

Stage 1 | Stage 2 | Stage 3

Figure 8.5 A blank table can be used as a graphic organizer to help students identify the *y*-intercept in a linear relationship. In this example, Stage 1 shows the original graphic organizer, Stage 2 shows how students might fill in the *x* values for the points they want to determine, and Stage 3 shows how students would transfer the information from the problem into the graphic organizer. Students could next use linear reasoning to determine the value of *y* when *x* is equal to zero.

what they already knew to gain more information. The teacher showed students how to organize their information differently to make the answer clearer.

Practice using the Graphic Organizer to Solve Problems

The graphic organizer in Figure 8.2 can assist in calculation, but it is only a tool to help students answer a question. Filling in the graphic organizer is not the goal of the task. Even when the table is completed, students must still identify the correct information to answer the question – in this case, the number of juniors and seniors in Coach Mesa's athletics class.

It is important to provide students with meaningful practice so they can become familiar with a graphic organizer's use. Teachers can provide problems intentionally designed to use the graphic organizer. This will help students understand its value. This should be followed up with spaced practice spread out over days and weeks to keep reviewing the skill. During this period, some students may become less dependent on the graphic organizer while others continue to rely on it heavily.

Help Students Identify When to Use the Graphic Organizer

In order to use a graphic organizer independently, students must understand when it is appropriate to use the tool. Students need to learn to recognize which sorts of problems are suited to a specific graphic organizer. During the early stages of instruction, teachers frequently give students the graphic organizer they will be using. This cues students to exactly the type of problem being solved. This may be a helpful early scaffold, but teachers should work toward helping students identify problem types on their own and selecting any tools which will be helpful.

Students who exhibit difficulties with math reasoning may need additional guidance in distinguishing different types of problems. For example, Pythagorean Theorem problems, proportional reasoning problems, and area problems may all feature triangles. Some students will need intentional practice identifying different types of problems and the skills necessary for each. Teachers can help students compare and contrast similar problems, noting the key differences. They can invite students to discuss sets of problems with a peer and sort them into categories. Teachers can model their own thinking as they work with students, for example, "I notice problems with similar figures always include more than one shape," or "I can see that there is not a right angle in this problem, so I doubt I can answer any questions using the Pythagorean Theorem." This is an important part of the instruction to help students effectively choose tools to use when solving problems and become more independent mathematicians.

Make the Graphic Organizer Easily Accessible

Graphic organizers are not only a tool for struggling learners. They help all students visualize mathematical relationships and categorize information. Some students may rely on these tools longer than others, but graphic organizers should be viewed as a resource and not as a crutch. To clearly send this message, in most cases, teachers should make sure all students are familiar with graphic organizers and their use. In cases where a graphic organizer is used with a small group of students (perhaps to address a learning gap from a previous grade level), teachers should emphasize it as a tool for a specific concept and not for specific students. It should not always be the same group of students working with graphic organizers. The groups should vary depending on the tool and student needs.

It is also important that graphic organizers are available to all students whenever practical. Students should be able to discreetly access these tools when they need them. There may be convenient ways to distribute graphic organizers digitally. Teachers can share a digital folder with all students that contains copies of the tools or post them in a learning management system where all students know how to access them.

Removing the Scaffolds

Graphic organizers are a form of scaffolding to support students as they are learning a new skill. When construction workers install scaffolding on a developing building, they anticipate the day they can remove the scaffolding so the building can stand on its own. Similarly, teachers of students with IEPs are anticipating what scaffolded supports they can remove as a developing student has outgrown the need for them.

In the early stages of instruction, it is appropriate to demonstrate the use of graphic organizers and support students in their use. Ideally, students will eventually create their own methods of organization as they are needed. If we picture the initial instruction and the eventual independent student work as opposite ends of a spectrum, there is a lot of room in between for teachers to help students grow and progress. Teachers can start with a detailed graphic organizer that includes several supports including instructions, labels, or color coding. As students become more familiar with its use, teachers can remove information, prompting students to use the tool more independently. Figure 8.6 shows an example of this progression using the circle graphic organizer from earlier in the chapter. As students become more comfortable with the graphic organizer as a tool, teachers can shift the burden of its construction onto students and expect students to effectively use it with less prompting. Some students will not progress to the stage where they can draw their own graphic organizer on a blank sheet of paper, but we work to help them get closer to that point (Fisher & Frey, 2018).

If teachers do not encourage students to become more independent in their use of graphic organizers, they risk stifling students' development of conceptual understanding. Students may grow to use the graphic organizer as a procedural crutch, forgetting the underlying concept it represents. The graphic organizer is not the end goal, but a tool for answering questions. In the example of the circle graphic organizer in Figure 8.6, student reasoning should extend past "add the three numbers from row 2 to get row 3." We want students to understand and remember "the circumference of a circle is roughly three times the length of its diameter." It is important that classroom conversations emphasize mathematical understanding and not simply completing the graphic organizer.

Math graphic organizers are tools to help students keep track of important information, understand the relationships between that information, or make a plan to use that information to answer questions. They allow us to support

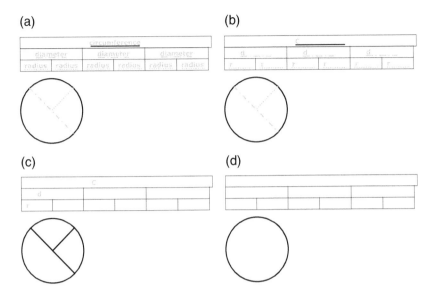

Figure 8.6 This sample progression demonstrates how a teacher might help students progress from an early version of a graphic organizer that includes several supports to later versions that rely on students to use the tool with increasing independence. Stage 1 in the sample progression color codes the circle and the recording area and labels the parts of a circle that students must identify. Stage 2 abbreviates the parts of a circle to continue providing a prompt for students. Stage 3 removes the color coding and expects students to connect the parts of a circle with the recording area on their own. Stage 4 is simply a blank table and circle diagram. Some students may progress past Stage 4 to the point where they can create the graphic organizer on their own if it is needed at all.

students as they strengthen their reasoning. If used appropriately, they help students make sense of the math they are using and justify their thinking as they solve problems. Many students will adapt these tools to their own needs and make them their own. Other students may continue using graphic organizers exactly as they were presented in class. For this second group, graphic organizers still allow students to reason mathematically and solve problems with conceptual understanding.

References

Fisher, D., & Frey, N. (2018). The uses and misuses of graphic organizers in content area learning. *Reading Teacher, 71*(6), 763–766. 10.1002/trtr.1693

Kelemanik, G., Lucenta, A., Creighton, S. J., & Lampert, M. (2016). *Routines for reasoning: Fostering the mathematical practices in all students.* Heinemann.

9   Memory and Retention

One recent spring semester, I spent two weeks working with a small group of eighth-grade students who had failed the state's end-of-course test and were preparing to attempt the test a second time. The group members were mostly boys who were not excited about attending an extra math period in the middle of their school day. We had managed to build a rapport over our time together, but many of them lacked confidence in their math skills and were easily frustrated. Each day we worked through activities that focused on conceptual understanding while keeping the students active. Our review tasks had us constantly moving around the room, matching cards, creating posters, or building geometric shapes.

One day we were exploring problems involving the volume of cylinders. This eighth-grade standard builds on prior knowledge about volume that students have been developing since elementary school. I decided to tap into that previous knowledge.

"Do you remember in fifth grade," I began.

Immediately a chorus of resistance started: "I don't remember anything." "That was a long time ago."

I plowed ahead without pausing. "When you learned about volume, your teacher …"

"We had a terrible teacher." "We didn't do anything in fifth grade."

"Your teacher had you take a box and you made a layer of little cubes across the bottom of the box." Everyone suddenly listened quietly. "Then you figured out how many layers of cubes it would take to fill up the whole box."

"Oh yeah," several heads started nodding. "We did do that!"

One of teachers' most common concerns about struggling math students is their ability to retain knowledge and skills. Many students qualify for special education services because of underlying issues with either short-term working memory or long-term storage and retrieval. This is significant for math learners. Our discipline uses words that students do not encounter in other places (hypotenuse, interquartile). We take words that are common and give them uncommon meanings (mean, origin, range). We also present so much new

DOI: 10.4324/9781003346333-13

information at such a rapid pace that it is essential to intentionally help students store information in their long-term memory and retrieve it when it's needed. It is important to intentionally help build students' memory and to help them prioritize the skills and knowledge they are storing to recall later.

Anchor Activities

Fortunately for the students in that "bonus" math class, their teachers had created an anchor activity. Their fifth-grade math lesson on the volume of prisms created a lasting memory that allowed these students to connect back to the essential concepts. Like a boat connected to an anchor, this memory was a fixed point that we could rely on.

This group of students struggled in math class. In fact, one could argue that these particular students were struggling more than any other eighth-grade math students on campus. But when we talked about this volume activity from three years ago, they all remembered. Suddenly we were able to discuss the base of a prism and how it connects to the circle that forms the base of a cylinder. My students were able to describe to their shoulder partners how the height of the cylinder would help them calculate the cylinder's volume. Our lesson on cylinders was no longer brand-new information to decipher, it was just an extension of something they had already learned years ago.

There are several reasons this moment was so successful. I had no idea who taught my students in fifth grade, but I trusted that the teacher(s) had covered this standard from the curriculum and had guided students through the hands-on exploration described in the state guidelines. That physical experience of filling a box with little cubes, counting the number of cubes in one layer, learning how each layer makes a part of the volume – that experience created an anchor point in each student's memory that we were able to connect to three years later. If that teacher had simply given students a formula to memorize, I doubt it would have stuck with them over all that time. If the fifth-grade teacher pointed to a picture of a prism and talked about the layers that make its volume, I do not believe my students' eyes would have lit up with recognition when I asked them to recall the event. But filling that box with cubes made a lasting impression.

Of course, filling a box with cubes can be a memorable experience by itself, but it was also important that this task was grounded in conceptual under-standing. Students weren't memorizing someone else's learning; they were constructing knowledge for themselves. They could explore the volume of a prism from multiple approaches. They could make conjectures and test them out. By discovering the relationship between a prism's base and its volume for themselves, that knowledge is more likely to be effectively stored in long-term memory for later use. Rote memorization of a formula or copying sample problems from a teacher's lecture builds fewer connections in the brain and is more difficult to recall later.

I am grateful to all the fifth-grade teachers who placed that anchor in my students' memory banks. My task now, in middle school, is to build on that work. If I don't connect our current classwork to that prior memory, I have not only squandered an opportunity to build on that prior knowledge, but I have increased my students' cognitive load. They feel as though they are learning several packets of disconnected information. When we connect to prior knowledge, however, we help students mentally organize information. We provide them with strategies to retrieve that information when they need it.

In this case, I knew how to tap into that memory because my middle school team spent time reading over the vertical alignment of the standards in each unit. I was able to be more specific than "In one of your math classes, you learned about the volume of a prism." I asked students to think back to a specific year and I described the general task they experienced. Maybe it was a small-group task, it might have been a teacher demonstration or even a video, but it happened in fifth grade, and it filled the bottom layer of a box with cubes.

This vertical alignment is especially important when teaching students with IEPs. By reviewing the prior grade-level skills that we will be building on, we are better prepared to recognize problem areas that students encounter during a unit. For example, students often spend several years developing concepts around the dimensions and area of rectangles, but a much shorter time discovering the geometric properties of triangles. The parts of a circle are generally introduced for the first time in the middle of middle school. It is not surprising, then, when I encounter students who have a strong grasp of the concept of area but struggle with the difference between radius and circumference. I can anticipate this challenge and I can prepare to address that gap when I see it. (In this case, I might have cards labeled with the parts of a circle for students to use at their desks. If a student needs more support, a short activity where we color code the dimensions of a circle might help as well.)

In summary, my students benefited because their prior teacher had implemented the curriculum, the curriculum encouraged conceptual understanding through strong visuals or hands-on manipulatives, and my team had prepared by reviewing the vertical alignment. Students with IEPs often struggle with memory and retention, and when we place these mental anchors and connect to them, it increases their retention.

As teachers, we can create those anchor activities as well. They will help students remember important concepts throughout the remainder of the year, and provide a connection point on which future teachers can build. There are a few components to remember when designing an anchor activity.

Choose a high-priority learning target. Not all middle school math concepts are equally important. One of our jobs as teachers is helping students recognize the big ideas in the curriculum. Like writing an outline, we want to create anchor activities around the major headings, then connect other minor topics back to that key idea. For example, we might plan an activity that helps students explore the concept of proportionality. We can then refer to that activity when we describe linear relationships, scale drawings, and percentages. If students understand that all of those concepts are just facets of proportional reasoning, they can apply all of their understanding of proportions to those topics.

Focus on conceptual learning. Anchor activities should be built around big ideas and not the "stuff" that makes all the details. When my students understood the relationship between the volume of a box and a number of cubes and layers that fit inside, I could help them apply that understanding to other prisms and cylinders. If they had only understood that the formula $V = lwh$ describes the volume of a rectangular prism, we could not have made the same connections. Additionally, conceptual understanding will stay constant as students' math knowledge grows. This is the information that truly is an anchor. We have all encountered students who mistakenly believe that you cannot subtract a larger number from a smaller number or that in the long division "the bigger number always goes inside the house." These procedural tricks may work for a short time, but they do not fit the math that students will learn as their experience grows. We want students to remember underlying concepts, such as "division breaks items into groups of equal size," or "numbers get smaller as we move to the left on a number line."

When I teach students the concept of functions, I emphasize the broad concept that each input value will produce only one output value. We explore some analogies to represent that definition. Each time I order "Combo #1" at my favorite fast food restaurant, I should be charged the same price. If "Combo #1" costs me $6 but costs another customer $4.50, someone is going to be upset. After we establish this idea, we apply this concept to different settings. We look at tables where each input has one output and other tables where some inputs have multiple outputs. Students can sort those tables according to our conceptual definition and make observations about the tables in each category. We can do the same for graphs, mapping diagrams, and lists of ordered pairs.

I do not start by describing the different representations of functions and non-functions. If I started with vertical line tests and looked for repeated x-values in a table, there would be two problems. First of all, my students would probably miss the important underlying idea: that each input value should only be matched to one output value, but secondly, my students would perceive several disconnected problems, each with their own set of rules. To tell if a graph is a function, I apply the vertical line test. To determine if a mapping diagram is a function I look for an arrow with two heads and one tail. To find out if a table is a function, I look for repeats in the left column. And so on. This increases the amount of information I expect students to remember. Instead, if they remember (and understand) that each input must match with only one output, they can apply that definition to multiple representations. Of course, it is our job as teachers to guide students as they apply that definition to multiple representations, but the more discovery we allow them to do, the more memorable the knowledge will be.

Maintain the anchor. Once we have created an anchor activity, use it. Make connections and keep them fresh in students' minds. Refer back to it multiple times. Point out when we are using the knowledge from an anchor activity. "This problem is similar to when we measured all the staircases on campus to learn which one was the steepest. What was different about the steeper staircases?" You are not only reinforcing that memory for students, but you are helping them understand why it is a priority by seeing the different ideas and problems it can connect with.

Neurodiversity and Memory

There are two distinct categories of memory: short-term (or working memory) and long-term. Students may struggle with one or both, and we support each category differently. Short-term memory is where students hold information as they do quick calculations or mental math. Most individuals can hold three to five pieces of information for several seconds, though this may be affected by stress, mood, or fatigue (Sousa, 2016). Students with below-average working memory may struggle to do the same mental math as their grade-level peers or forget what operation they were doing before they have finished working out a problem. Decoding lengthy problems may be especially challenging for students in this group, and distracting information or unnecessary facts may clog their working memory and make it difficult for them to solve problems. Alternately, students may struggle with storing and retrieving information from long-term memory. We see this when a student struggles to complete tasks they were able to do a few days ago or continues to forget vocabulary they have been exposed to for years. Different strategies may be effective for each group of students.

As we mentioned before, conceptual instruction and prioritizing a few key concepts will minimize the memory demands on students. For students with long-term memory issues, the issue is not just placing items in their memory, but recovering those memories on demand, a process called *retrieval*. This is why we establish connections between problems, skills, and concepts to help students tap into and retrieve the information they have stored in long-term memory. It is helpful to create opportunities for students to practice retrieving that information from their memory. We want to revisit concepts regularly over increasing periods of time, in what is called spaced practice (Hattie et al., 2017). If we provide intense one-day practice on a particular skill, students are less likely to remember that skill than if they practiced a few problems spaced out over several occasions. We want to revisit a skill right when students are about to forget it – perhaps a day or two after it was introduced, then a week later, then a few weeks later. This goal is to increase the amount of time between the review, but the length of these intervals will depend on the particular student's need.

Spaced practice also helps students recognize the key components of a problem when they must recall what skills they are using for a particular question. When we focus our practice on one particular skill at a time, we do not give them an opportunity to develop their problem-solving skills. They know this problem will require them to identify a ratio and multiply because all the problems on this page have been about identifying ratios and multiplying. Deciding whether a problem with triangles is asking them to find area, hypotenuse, or a scale factor, helps them become better problem solvers and helps them mentally organize those concepts.

Mnemonic devices can be helpful for recalling specific factual information. Math class comes with some unfamiliar vocabulary. For example, many middle schoolers confuse the terms *numerator* and *denominator* though they may remember that they are both parts of a fraction. Remembering that "Denominator and Down both start with D" can help students correctly use those terms until the information becomes more permanent.

In his meta-analysis of educational research, John Hattie and colleagues (2017) conclude that mnemonics are less effective than spaced practice at improving students' memory, and they should be limited to factual information. Using mnemonics to recall a procedural algorithm can deemphasize the mathematics behind the calculation and may result in students misunderstanding the algorithm or applying it in situations where it is not appropriate.

Students with short-term memory disorders may have difficulty completing calculations as they struggle to hold items in working memory. In these cases, it is often appropriate to teach students to use a calculation aid such as a number chart, multiplication chart, or calculator. It is important that we teach students how to use these aids. We may also adjust our classroom tasks to accommodate the student's level of ability. By modifying the numbers in a problem or chunking a task into digestible steps, students may be able to access the same general task as their peers. For students with limited working memory, the distracting information contained in many math problems can be overwhelming. We can limit these distractions in new instruction, and then help students to develop strategies to identify and ignore this information as their new skills develop.

Students with short-term or long-term memory concerns can both benefit from the implementation of graphic organizers as a place to record information and organize that information in a way that makes sense of the mathematical relationships that are present. The graphic organizer in Figure 9.1 helps students apply the relationships between the radius, diameter, and circumference of a circle.

The organizer in Figure 9.2 depicts the relationship between the sides of a right triangle. For any right triangle, if you construct a square adjacent to each side of the triangle, the area of the two smaller squares will sum to the area of the largest square.

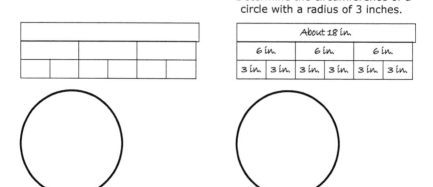

Figure 9.1 This graphic organizer displays the relationship between the measurements of a circle. The lower row is made up of 6 horizontal strips that each represent the length of a circle's radius. The middle row contains strips that are each twice as long as the radius. These strips each represent the length of the circle's diameter. The top strip is slightly longer than three diameters, and this strip represents the circle's circumference. This graphic organizer helps students use one measurement of a circle to determine any of the other measurements.

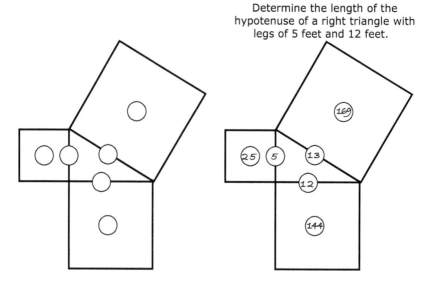

Figure 9.2 This graphic organizer includes a right triangle and squares placed adjacent to each side. There are recording areas on each side of the triangle and within each square, for students to fill in measurements. The area of the largest square (located in the top right) is equal to the area of the two smaller squares. Students can use just a few pieces of information and the relationships represented in this diagram to determine the remaining pieces of information.

I once used this graphic organizer when I pulled a small group of students during class to review finding the missing side of a right triangle. I drew this graphic organizer on a small whiteboard and filled in two of the numbers. I then asked the students to take turns filling in any measurement they knew until the entire diagram was complete. The only rule was that they could only write one number before passing the marker to another student. It was delightful to watch as students competed to quickly fill in the first few circles before pondering what else they could determine. Usually, after a pause, one student would recognize a connection and a new flurry of activity would erupt as that unlocked more clues. Finding all the values in the diagram took minimal prompting on my part. After a few practice rounds, we read word problems together and used the descriptions in the problems to fill in all the parts of the organizer. This simple diagram helped students keep track of what they knew but also reminded them of what other information they could deduce.

Both of these graphic organizers provide a way for students to collect the information they know and extend that information to solve problems. Both of these examples support students' reasoning as they leverage mathematical relationships.

Vocabulary

Academic vocabulary in math classes can be a challenge for many students. Neurodiverse students may have additional challenges in this area due to long-term memory issues, deficits in verbal reasoning, or other concerns. As teachers, it is important to help students gain and retain the vocabulary necessary to be successful in our classes.

As with skills and concepts, vocabulary instruction is most effective when it is connected to other knowledge. Whenever possible, vocabulary should be introduced in context. It is ineffective to present students with several unfamiliar vocabulary words at the beginning of a unit of study when they do not understand what these words describe or how they will be used. Instead, vocabulary can be used to formalize a concept students have already discovered.

For example, an eighth-grade class I visited had student groups engaged in a task where they were designing squares of different sizes. The assignment asked students to use grid paper to draw squares with a specified area: 25 square units, 100 square units, and 50 square units. The problems were designed to become more challenging as students progressed. Most students could mentally guess and check that a square with an area of 25 square units would have a side length of 5 units. After some false starts, they determined a side length of 10 units would produce a square with an area of 100 square units. Most groups were stumped when challenged to produce a square with an area of 50 square units. The teacher encouraged students to persist in exploring the problem.

"Try some rough drafts on your grid paper and see if they work," she encouraged one group. Visiting another group, she observed, "I see that you drew a rectangle with sides of 5 units and 10 units. That does give you an area of 50, but can you change your rectangle to make it a square?"

When a third group was showing signs of frustration, she adjusted the task. "Can you tell me a square that's too small and a square that's too big?"

When the class debriefed the task, she asked students to describe some of their early attempts.

"First we tried dividing the area by two," one student explained. "That didn't work, so we tried dividing by four since there are four sides, but when we made that square, it wasn't right either."

The teacher facilitated the conversation as students established that they could not identify a straightforward calculation to determine the side length of a square given its area, but they knew they were trying to identify a number they could multiply by itself to equal the area.

Then the teacher formalized this notion with vocabulary. "We have a word for that. The *square root* of 50 is the number we can multiply by itself to equal 50." Then she posted a sentence frame with an example at the front of the room, shown in Figure 9.3.

Students now had a way to remember the term square root because they needed a word for this relationship and they practiced using it in context. In fact, this task allowed students to review some geometry concepts and problem-solve as a group, but the primary objective of this task was to help students learn the vocabulary word they would be using over the next few weeks.

Vocabulary instruction often divides words into three general tiers of vocabulary. Tier I words are words that we encounter in everyday conversation. Students have probably heard these words before. This might include words like volume, measure, height, or representation. We typically address these words as they come up. We read a task together with a group and ask students to paraphrase the assignment to determine whether we need to clarify any terms.

Tier II words are not content-specific, but we do not hear them in regular conversation. We may encounter words like experiment, dimensions, or scale

The square root of 16 is 4.

Because 4 × 4 is 16.

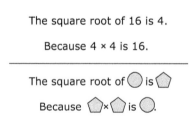

Figure 9.3 This sentence frame helped formalize students' understanding of the vocabulary term "square root."

more often in writing than in spoken language. We often pre-teach these words. I might tell a class that today's activity will ask them to conduct an experiment 10 times. In this case, the word "experiment" means the specific event they are recording, such as flipping a coin or spinning a spinner.

Finally, Tier III words are unique to a specific content area. These are words that we want to teach in context to formalize student learning. This category might include math terms like isosceles, denominator, or exponent. Once students have a need for this term, we can present it and its definition and provide some practice around the word.

If we want students to build fluency with academic vocabulary, they must have several opportunities to interact with a word, using it in context (Beck & McKeown, 2013). The cards in Figure 9.4 can be used in several different ways to give students multiple meaningful exposures to the terms.

Initially, students can simply match the vocabulary term with the definition or representation. This is a short task that can be completed at a station or as a brief warm-up task at the beginning of class. Later, the teacher can remove one or two cards from the set and challenge students to create the missing term or definition on a blank index card. Finally, students can be divided into two groups. One group has the first set of cards (constant, radius, volume, and pyramid), while the other group has the second set of cards (coefficient,

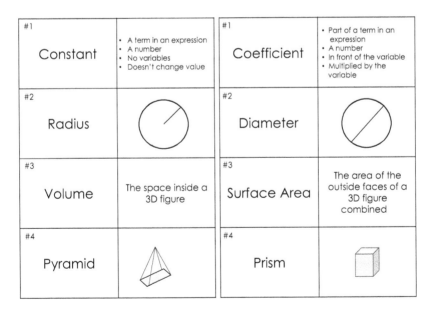

Figure 9.4 This single set of cards can be used in multiple ways to allow students to practice using academic vocabulary with minimal teacher preparation.

diameter, surface area, and prism). Once students have matched their cards, the teacher asks students to partner with a member of the other group and match up cards with the same number (constant with coefficient, and so on). Students should spend a few minutes discussing the cards in each set and how they are alike or different.

This single set of cards can be used in multiple activities. This means there is minimal setup for the teacher, but students can have several opportunities to work with the vocabulary terms. This is one way to create spaced practice allowing students to store and retrieve information from memory.

The right instructional strategies can support students who struggle with memory and recall. First, as teachers, we need to identify the key concepts that are worth remembering and prioritize them. When we teach those concepts by focusing on conceptual understanding instead of details and special cases, we reduce students' memory load. Next, we can design anchor activities around these topics. Design memorable tasks that help students observe the underlying math concepts and connect it with their pre-existing knowledge. Continue to maintain these mental anchors by referring to them frequently and connecting them to new information. Finally, create opportunities for students to practice retrieving and using prior knowledge through intentional spaced practice. As the students in my "bonus" math class showed me, when we invest in these instructional strategies, our students continue to benefit for years to come.

References

Beck, I. L., & McKeown, M. G. (2013). *Bringing words to life*. The Guilford Press.

Hattie, J., Fisher, D., Frey, N., Gojak, L. M., Moore, S. D., & Mellman, W. (2017). *Visible learning for mathematics: What works best to optimize student learning, grades K-12*. Corwin Mathematics.

Sousa, D. A. (2016). *How the special needs brain learns*. Sage.

10 Questioning

One amazing team of teachers I worked with developed an efficient system for delivering targeted, differentiated instruction for their students. Every few days, the three teachers would each plan a separate task designed to address a different aspect of the same central learning goal. Usually, one lesson allowed students to practice the skill in new situations while the other two addressed specific misconceptions and provided some version of a scaffolded reteach. In order to determine which lesson each student should receive, the teachers created short exit tickets with two or three questions. Then after class, I was amazed at how quickly these teachers divided the exit tickets into three separate piles based of student responses. Each pile corresponded to a different lesson, and the next day the teachers would divide up their classes of students to match the sorted exit tickets.

One day I watched one of these teachers sorting exit tickets rather quickly until she set one of the student papers aside. She showed me that the student's work was hard to follow, but it looked like they had arrived at the correct answer. Looking at the paper, I was undecided as to which class group would be the best placement for this student. I asked the teacher how she could tell which differentiated lesson was most appropriate for the student.

"It's no big deal," she told me. "I'll catch them right before class tomorrow and ask them a couple of questions about their work. Based on their answers, I can tell if they need the reteach or if they're ready for some extended practice."

The teacher's solution made perfect sense, but it had not originally occurred to me. She planned to tap into a wealth of information by simply talking to the student themself and asking a few questions.

Questions are one of the most powerful tools in any teacher's arsenal, but in many cases, they are underutilized. Teachers can unlock a wealth of information about their students by asking carefully crafted questions and listening to student answers. However, research suggests teacher talk fills almost 90% of class time (Hattie at al., 2017) and teachers' wait time – the pause teachers allow students to think before rephrasing or answering their own question – is typically less than a second (Ingram & Elliott, 2016). Changing that dynamic and using more quality

DOI: 10.4324/9781003346333-14

questioning in the classroom helps teachers better monitor their students' academic progress and push students' thinking to the next level.

Two of the primary purposes for questions in the classroom are to assess student understanding or to advance student thinking. These categories of assessing and advancing questions both play an important role in the classroom, and they may look slightly different for students with IEPs.

Assessing questions are like the ones my colleagues asked to divide students into the appropriate learning groups. They are questions designed so a teacher can gather information about what students know or how they are thinking about a situation. The point of an assessing question is to hear the answer. Teachers are usually looking for specific responses and may even design interventions or follow-up tasks depending on how a student responds. Assessing questions focus on what a student already knows. They help teachers gauge where students are now, and where they are ready to go next.

Assessing questions are written around clear learning targets. They measure specific knowledge and skills. Table 10.1 contains some examples of assessing questions.

Each of these questions is directly related to the learning target. These questions could be used as part of a pre-assessment to see what students already know, or they could help a teacher determine how effective instruction on these learning targets has been. Test questions are the most literal example of assessing questions, but effective teachers constantly use questions to informally gather information about where students are in their knowledge development.

Assessing questions are a powerful tool for gathering information about students, but teachers should keep in mind the unique characteristics of students with IEPs. Some students may not respond as quickly or thoroughly as teachers

Table 10.1 Assessing questions like these are a tool for teachers to gauge students' current level of understanding

---

Learning Target: The student will determine the area and perimeter of triangles.

Potential Assessing Questions:
- What is the area of a triangle with a base length of 5 inches and a height of 3 inches?
- What are some possible dimensions of an obtuse triangle with an area of 24 square centimeters?

Learning Target: The student will identify key features of quadratic functions.

Potential Assessing Questions:
- What are the zeros of the function $y = 2x^2 - 12x + 10$?
- Does the function $y = x^2 + 7x + 12$ have a maximum or a minimum?

Learning Target: The student will calculate the distance between two points on the coordinate plane.

Potential Assessing Questions:
- What is the distance between the points $(-3, 5)$ and $(2, 7)$?
- How far is the point $(-6, -2)$ from the origin?

---

expect, even though the student knows the content. It can be appropriate to adapt the manner of questioning to the student.

Students with an SLD in verbal expression or written expression may struggle to adequately respond to questions, particularly when pressed for an immediate answer. In many circumstances, teachers can give students a preview of the questions that will be asked or provide students with time to practice their responses by writing their responses or discussing their answers with a partner.

If students struggle with listening comprehension, teachers should look for supplemental ways to share verbal questions. In addition to sharing a question aloud, projecting it on a screen or including it on notes at a student's desk may help. Additionally, it may be necessary to review challenging vocabulary or clarify similar words that sound alike (like "independent" and "dependent"). Allowing extra processing time before answering a question is often beneficial. It is important for teachers to protect that processing time by reminding students not to blurt out responses during this thinking time.

Think-Write-Pair-Share is a protocol that gives students processing time to respond to a prompt and helps them practice their communication skills. It is a strategy that can benefit many students, but particularly those who need extra processing time or have IEP goals related to communication skills. The process begins with the teacher asking a question or giving a prompt (such as a short video). Students are given a predetermined amount of time to independently think about their responses and write down their thoughts. Sometimes teachers may ask for formal writing with complete sentences, other times they may be looking for a few notes or key ideas that students can refer to later. This may be a good time to provide sentence stems for specific students to guide their responses or help them get started.

After students have had time to record some thoughts, they meet with a partner and discuss what they have written. When students first engage in this protocol, it is important to teach students how to take turns sharing and listening. Teachers may model or provide scripts for students to use until they are comfortable sharing their responses and listening to their partner's responses. For students with communication difficulties, this is an opportunity to hear how another student expresses themself. They get to hear math content knowledge being shared and vocabulary being used in context. Then students get to practice communicating in a low-stakes setting. It is often easier to share briefly with a peer than to speak with a teacher or share when the entire class is listening.

The final step of this protocol is a whole-class discussion where some students share their responses with the class. This allows students to hear from more than just a single partner. Teachers can guide this conversation by intentionally selecting comments that were overheard during the partner share.

Strategies like Think-Write-Pair-Share can be adapted to the needs of individual learners. With planning and adaptation, this may be part of a student's SDI to help them meet IEP goals. The strategy can also be adjusted according to time constraints or instructional goals. Teachers may skip the writing portion of the protocol or have students mix themselves into new pairs a few times before sharing out in the class discussion. Depending on the needs of the specific learners in the classroom, a teacher may choose to have a small group of students partner with the teacher while the rest of the class discusses in pairs. The strategy is flexible, and teachers should consider the ability and goals of their specific students.

For students with below-average fluid reasoning, assessing knowledge through questions can pose different challenges. Teachers often try to determine the depth of a student's conceptual understanding by asking unconventional questions. Figure 10.1 shows an example of a question that asks students to apply their knowledge of the Pythagorean theorem.

For students who struggle to apply their knowledge in novel situations, this line of questioning may place them at a disadvantage. Depending upon the student's specific needs, it may be appropriate to scaffold the question or balance novel tasks with questions that directly assess the desired skill. While reasoning and application are essential parts of the secondary math curriculum, questions like the one shown in Figure 10.2 can show whether a student understands the underlying skill.

Students who struggle with fluid reasoning may have an IEP goal around problem-solving and applying math skills. Intentional practice and well-planned SDI can improve a student's ability to address novel questions, but balanced assessment questions will provide a more complete picture of student skills and knowledge.

The sport field shown in the diagram is shaped like a rectangle. Alex ran the length of the field from point A to point B. Chris ran diagonally across the field from point A to point C. How much farther did Chris run?

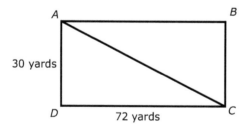

Figure 10.1 This sample question can reveal a student's understanding of the Pythagorean theorem by asking them to apply it in a novel setting. Without adequate practice, questions like this one can disadvantage students who struggle with fluid reasoning.

What is the length of the longest side of this right triangle?

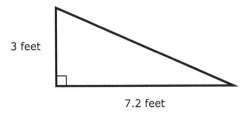

3 feet

7.2 feet

Figure 10.2 This question directly assesses a student's ability to apply the Pythagorean Theorem to determine the length of a missing side of a right triangle.

If assessing questions help determine what a student knows and where they are ready to go next, *advancing* questions are used to help push students to that next step. They are questions designed to help students think. If you have ever responded to a student's question by asking another question of your own, you probably asked an advancing question. Advancing questions are based on the current learning target, but they also take into consideration the student's current task and their level of readiness. Teachers may anticipate some advancing questions they may use during class, but they can be harder to script in advance than assessing questions. Table 10.2 includes examples of some advancing questions.

Each of these questions is an instructional tool to facilitate the task at hand. The teacher is not expecting a specific answer, but rather the teacher intends for the question to prompt a new line of inquiry. This is not prior knowledge, and the teacher will not assess the student with their response. This question is a way to tap into students' curiosity and build new knowledge as students try to determine the answer. It is interesting to notice that these same questions could often become assessing questions in later coursework but at this point in the student's development, these are advancing questions.

Just as teachers differentiate classroom instruction, sometimes advancing questions must be adjusted to the specific student or student group. Students with IEPs may need some scaffolds or direction as they explore advancing questions. While teachers may adapt their questions to guide a student's discovery, students should be allowed to reason and explore as much as they are able. Replacing advancing questions with directive statements or class notes will have a harmful impact on students' learning. It can be much more effective to help students develop mathematical properties on their own instead of stating those properties for students to memorize. As students discover mathematical properties, they form connections to prior knowledge and lay the groundwork for future exploration. Students tend to retain the information longer and understand it at a deeper level. This exploration – even when

Table 10.2 Advancing questions like those shown here are instructional tools to push student thinking forward

---

Learning Target: The student will determine the area and perimeter of triangles.

Task: Students are creating triangles and trading them with group members to determine the area and perimeter of each other's triangles

Potential Advancing Question:
• I see that you created a triangle with an area of 18 square centimeters. Can you design other triangles with the same area?

The teacher anticipates students will explore this question and it may provide an opportunity to observe that the area of a triangle depends only on the lengths of its base and height.

Learning Target: The student will identify key features of quadratic functions.

Task: Students are graphing quadratic functions and identifying the zeros, line of symmetry, and maximum or minimum.

Potential Advancing Question:
• If you multiply all the terms of your quadratic function by the same factor, which key features will change?

The teacher wants students to observe that multiplying by a constant factor does change the graph of the function.

Learning Target: The student will calculate the distance between two points on the coordinate plane.

Task: Students are plotting points on the coordinate plane and applying the Pythagorean theorem to find the distance between the points by drawing a right triangle with vertices at the given points.

Potential Advancing Question:
• Do we have to plot the points every time? Is there a way we can determine the lengths of the triangle' legs without drawing it?

The teacher intends for students to discuss this question and develop the distance formula by noticing they can subtract x-values and y-values to calculate the lengths of the triangle's legs.

---

scaffolded – generates different types of brain activity compared to when students are told facts or taught to replicate skills. Mathematical exploration and discovery are typically more engaging and often lead to greater success in future math courses (Baroody et al., 2009).

Instead of removing the reasoning and exploration, teachers can provide support for students depending on their current ability. Often students with IEPs will need more time to reason than their grade-level peers. Teachers can look for opportunities to provide this time by prioritizing standards and helping students focus their time on vital learning targets. Some students may be able to forego certain practice assignments or warm-up tasks so they can spend more time on a reasoning activity. Teachers may formatively assess specific students with one or two verbal questions that can be answered more quickly than completing an exit ticket.

As teachers help students focus their class time on the most useful tasks, it is important to notice when assignments can be shortened. It is not always important for students to *finish* a task or worksheet, but teachers should have clear ways to measure when a student has achieved the goal of the task. Sometimes that looks like a list of assessing questions. When a student can answer those questions successfully, they are ready to move on to another activity. After a certain point, a student's time is better spent on a new task than on repetitive practice. (Though spaced practice at some point in the future can help solidify learning.)

Other times, a reasoning task may need to be chunked into manageable pieces. Teachers may also introduce graphic organizers or manipulatives to facilitate reasoning or to help draw students' attention to the patterns and relationships teachers want them to notice. In the example question about the distance formula, teachers might create right triangles on transparencies or tracing paper so students can observe the isolated triangle, then place the triangle on a piece of grid paper to notice the relationship between the side lengths and the unit squares on the coordinate grid. This may be an intermediary step as students move from counting squares on the coordinate grid to calculating the length of the triangle's legs by subtracting x- and y-values.

Teachers should carefully gauge their advancing questions to the specific student's level of success and frustration. If teachers are pushing too far or too fast, students may retreat or shut down. When this starts to happen, sometimes teachers can implement additional scaffolds, but other times it may be more useful to pivot to a different task for a short period of time.

Advancing questions can be further categorized into two groups: *funneling* questions and *focusing* questions (Hagenah et al. 2018). Funneling questions are leading questions that very directly guide students as they solve a problem or work through a situation. The questions are designed to walk students through a process, often with little attention to the thinking that is happening.

Focusing questions, by contrast, place the cognitive load on the student. They help a student work through a problem by making connections to information they already know or pointing out potential areas of conflict. Focusing questions are intended to help students reason through their work and model questions they might ask themselves in future situations. Consider the examples of focusing and funneling questions in Table 10.3.

In the examples of funneling questions, the teacher is really directing the student, but in the form of questions. The questions ask students how they would complete each new step of the problem. The example focusing questions encourage students to make connections. They ask students what they mean when they say two figures are the "same shape." They ask students how numbers in a proportion are related. The teacher might ask different focusing questions if a student seemed to be moving in a different direction. These questions are intended to help a student build from what they know now.

Table 10.3 The funneling questions shown here walk students through a rote solution process step-by-step. The focusing questions, however, suggest ways that students can use what they already know to approach this problem

Triangle *DEF* is similar to triangle *GHI*.

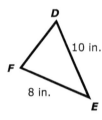
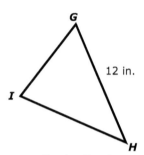

Funneling Questions

Teacher: What tool do we use to find the missing side in a pair of similar shapes?

Students: A proportion

T: How will we label the two ratios in this proportion?

S: Um? Top and bottom?

T: We could do that. What's another way we could label them?

S: Left triangle and right triangle?

T: Yes, or small triangle and large triangle. What numbers will we write in the ratio for the small triangle?

S: 8 and 10.

T: (Writes 8 over 10 on the board) And Which side do we know from the large triangle?

S: 12?

T: Yes, so do we write that next to the 8 or the 10?

S: Next to the 10.

T: Look at what the numbers have in common.

S: No, next to the 12.

T: (Writes 12 over x next to the original ratio.) Now solve this proportion for our missing value.

Focusing Questions

Teacher: The problem says these triangles are similar. What does that mean to you?

Student: They are the same shape, but different sizes. One is bigger than the other.

T: When you say these triangles are the same shape, what do you mean by that?

S: They look alike. The angles at each of the corners are the same.

T: What about the sides? If this side is twice as big, what do I know about that side?

S: It's also twice as big.

T: Yes, what word do we use to describe that?

S: The sides of the triangles are proportional to each other.

T: Now, looking at these triangles, the large one isn't twice as big. How can we compare them?

S: A proportion?

T: Yes, how do we know where to place numbers within a proportion?

S: The adjacent numbers correspond to each other. Like the small sides go next to each other or the top sides go next to each other.

T: Great. Show me what that might look like, then go ahead and find the missing value in your proportion.

In a typical classroom, there will be a balance between focusing and funneling questions. When working with students with IEPs, that balance may look different, but teachers should still provide as much opportunity for student sense-making as possible through focusing questions. When students explore and discover information on their own, it has a much stronger lasting impact than when students are passive recipients of the information. The modern secondary math classroom should prioritize reasoning and problem-solving, and the right forms of questions can be a powerful tool toward those goals.

References

Baroody, A. J., Bajwa, N. P., & Eiland, M. (2009). Why can't Johnny remember the basic facts? *Developmental Disabilities Research Reviews, 15*(1), 69–79. 10.1002/ddrr.45

Hagenah, S., Colley, C., & Thompson, J. (2018). Funneling versus focusing: When talk, tasks, and tools work together to support students' collective sensemaking. *Science Education International, 29*(4), 261–266.

Hattie, J., Fisher, D., & Frey, N. (2017). *Visible learning for mathematics: What works best to optimize student learning.* Corwin Mathematics.

Ingram, & Elliott, V. (2016). A critical analysis of the role of wait time in classroom interactions and the effects on student and teacher interactional behaviours. *Cambridge Journal of Education, 46*(1), 37–53. 10.1080/0305764X.2015.1009365

11 Manipulatives

It is not unusual to find myself working with a math student when they abruptly stop and ask me, "Is it alright if I use my fingers?" Of course, it is alright, I typically encourage students to use a wide range of tools if they will help them understand the task at hand. Our fingers are some of the oldest and most-used math manipulatives available. When students are asking permission to count on their fingers, it makes me wonder what messages they have received about math, what it means to be good at math, and the use of manipulatives in math. These students may feel that counting on their fingers is somehow cheating, but more likely, they falsely believe tools like these are juvenile and should be avoided. This is a troublesome reputation that manipulatives have earned in the math classroom. I have seen students resist working with colored counters or algebra tiles because they believe those items are only used by struggling students. As teachers, we must help our students understand that math manipulatives are a helpful resource for making sense of math. Some students may achieve a level of fluency that allows them to forgo using manipulatives for some types of problems, but not everyone will. And that is okay, too. And, by the way, I still sometimes use my fingers to count.

In early grades, math manipulatives support the development of arithmetic skills. Concrete objects help students visualize the process of *counting on* or *dividing into equal groups*. Elementary math classrooms are often filled with physical manipulatives such as counting bears, pattern blocks, clocks, or base-10 blocks. These tools not only help students observe mathematical relationships in a concrete context, but they also allow teachers to observe students' thought processes. As students work with manipulatives, it helps teachers see the mathematical connections happening within the student's mind.

In secondary math classrooms, as the context becomes more abstract, manipulatives can still provide a connection to concrete properties and help students develop an understanding of math concepts. In fact, as the concepts become more complicated, so do the math manipulatives that represent those concepts. At the very least, secondary math students should be taught to use integer chips, algebra tiles, and fraction bars, and they should have opportunities to explore

DOI: 10.4324/9781003346333-15

geometric properties with area tiles, physical nets, solids, and connecting polygons. Presenting these tools to all students improves understanding and helps diminish any stigma associated with using manipulatives. The next few pages describe some of the high-impact manipulatives that should be included in secondary math curricula.

Common Math Manipulatives

Integer chips (shown in Figure 11.1) are typically round, reversible counters that are yellow on one side and red on the other. Each chip represents a unit. The yellow side represents a positive unit and the red side represents a negative unit. Students can develop an understanding of integer operations as they use the chips to represent combining and removing integers.

Teachers use integer chips to develop the concept of a zero-pair that forms when an integer is combined with its additive inverse. This concept of the zero-pair becomes important in later work when students solve one-variable equations by combining constants or variables with their additive inverse. It is important to develop this concept with integers that represent concrete values so that students can apply this same reasoning to abstract variables when solving one-variable equations.

Fraction bars and fractions circles (shown in Figure 11.2) both help students compare fractions and mixed numbers as well as perform some fraction operations. Each tool has its benefits. Fraction circles can be helpful when comparing fractions because all circles are proportional to each other. We know what a

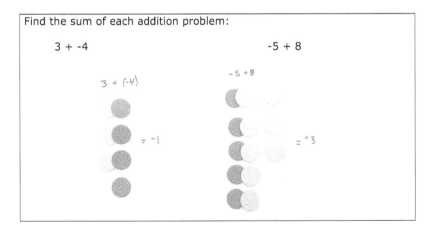

Figure 11.1 Two-color counters (or integer chips) help students observe properties of integers and develop an understanding of integer operations. It is particularly important for students to develop the concept of a zero-pair when a value is combined with its additive inverse.

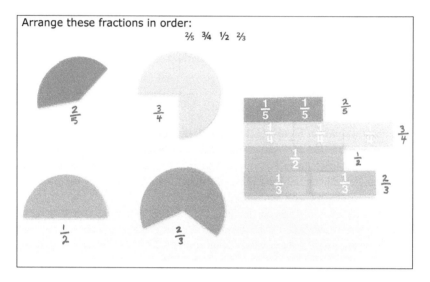

Figure 11.2 Fraction bars and fraction circles can help students to compare fractions and perform some simple operations with fractions.

whole circle looks like, so it is easy to recognize one-half of a circle or one-quarter of a circle. Fraction bars compare rectangular shapes, and we can only recognize one-half or one-quarter of a rectangle by comparing it to a unit rectangle. However, rectangles are often easier to draw, and most students find it difficult to hand draw a diagram representing a circle evenly divided into an odd number of pieces. As students begin representing fractions by drawing their own diagrams, most students find it much easier to divide a rectangle into equal pieces than to divide a circle.

In either case, students can compare fraction parts and combine multiple fractions together. Students can arrange pieces to see how many one-sixths it takes to equal one-half. It is also possible to represent some simple fraction operations such as multiplying a fraction by a whole number. Operations with these manipulatives become cumbersome, but they are valuable to help students create a mental model of fractions and comparison. For example, they visibly correct the common misconception that one-third is greater than one-fourth.

Algebra tiles (shown in Figure 11.3) extend students' understanding of integer operations to include variables. The tiles are reversible (just like integer chips) and there are tiles to represent a positive or negative integer one as well as tiles to represent a positive or negative variable x. Students can develop properties of balanced one-variable equations by working with algebra tiles. They learn that adding or removing the same value from both sides of the equation

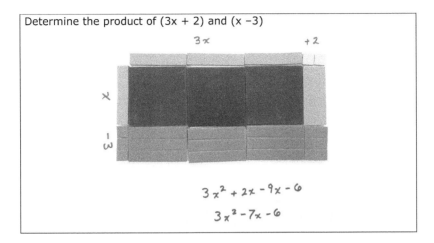

Determine the product of (3x + 2) and (x −3)

$$3 x^2 + 2x - 9x - 6$$
$$3 x^2 - 7x - 6$$

Figure 11.3 Algebra tiles are used to represent integer values and variables. They help students understand the concept of balancing an equation and they are commonly used to illustrate the factors of a quadratic expression using an area model.

maintains balance, as does multiplying or dividing each side by the same factor. Students apply the earlier concept of zero pairs to variables in order to efficiently solve one-variable equations.

There is also an algebra tile that represents a positive or negative x2, used when working with quadratic expressions. Students can use these extended algebra tiles to factor quadratic expressions by arranging the terms into a rectangle and applying the area model of multiplication to identify the factors as the length and width of the rectangle they created.

Secondary math teachers seem to continuously find new applications for colored tiles (shown in Figure 11.4). These squares are typically available in four different colors. They can be used to observe the area and perimeter of some basic shapes and to illustrate proportional relationships. Students can use the tiles to build simple patterns, and they are useful to demonstrate the probability of simple and compound events.

Interlocking cubes (shown in Figure 11.5) are a versatile tool for secondary math classrooms. They have many of the advantages of colored tiles, and they can be joined together to form small structures. They can be shaped into many geometric solids, allowing students to explore surface area and volume. They are available in many colors, making them convenient counters or representative props when acting out problems. Interlocking cubes can also be used to explore proportional reasoning. For example, teachers can challenge students to create different lines of cubes to represent "20% blue" or "one-third red."

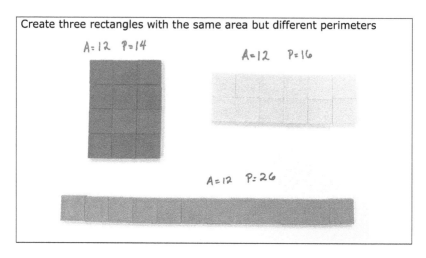

Figure 11.4 Colored tiles can be used as geometric tiles and as reasoning tools. Students can explore the area and perimeter or use the tiles to represent a variety of elements in math problems.

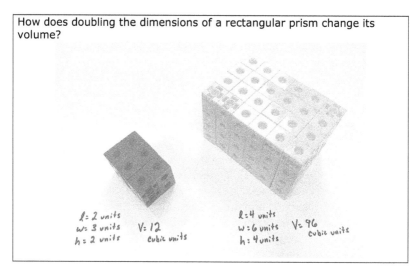

Figure 11.5 Interlocking cubes can be used to explore ratio and proportion, and students can create small geometric solids by joining them together.

Geometric solids and folding nets (shown in Figure 11.6) help students explore the properties of geometric figures. Students can handle three-dimensional representations of common solids to understand characteristics such as the difference between prisms and pyramids. Viewing folding nets allows students to notice what

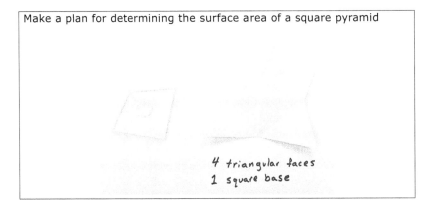

Make a plan for determining the surface area of a square pyramid

4 triangular faces
1 square base

Figure 11.6 Geometric solids and folding nets are helpful to demonstrate geometric relationships and develop concepts of volume, faces, and surface area.

figures comprise the surface area of geometric solids. Teachers can create experiences to demonstrate the relationship between the volume of geometric solids. For
example, by filling solids with water, students can observe that the volume of
a cone is one-third the volume of a cylinder with the same dimensions.

Effective Practices

It is important to teach students how to use math manipulatives. Students should
have time to become familiar with the object and then learn what they represent,
how they work together, and how they can be used to make sense of math
relationships.

When first introducing a new manipulative, give students some time to
explore them. If they work together in some way, like interlocking cubes or
connecting geometric shapes, allow students to see how they interact. Then,
explain how the manipulative will be used as a math tool. Teachers should
be explicit about what each manipulative represents. Remind students, for
example, that the small yellow square algebra tile represents the integer 1 and
the long red rectangular tile represents the variable -x. Many teachers post a
legend on the wall or on students' desks for easy reference. Teachers should
also be as consistent as possible when assigning meaning to manipulatives. If
a student, for example, is modeling a problem and using red square tiles to
represent the number of pizzas in the problem, it would be disruptive to switch
to using a different color or a different item to represent pizzas. At least in the
early stages, explicitly describe what each manipulative represents and avoid
using the same item in different contexts.

Teachers should then teach how the manipulative is used to model mathematical properties. This is not the time for teaching procedural rules about integers,

balancing equations, or calculating areas. Instead, teachers should demonstrate how the manipulative connects with problems we may solve. Teachers can show how to represent the equation $3x + 4 = 2x + 7$ with algebra tiles or students can practice combining integer chips to represent the problem $-4 + 7$. Intentionally design incremental practice that allows students to discover new features of the manipulative or move to more complicated applications as they are ready.

Teach all students how to use a manipulative and make them easily accessible to everyone in the class. Manipulatives are intended to help students make sense of mathematics and demonstrate their thinking. They are a tool for all learners, though individual students will vary in how and when they use manipulatives. Many students will likely develop more efficient methods for doing their math work without manipulatives, but the tools should still be available to everyone. We would not discourage a student who asks for a paper to work out their math or write down their thinking. In the same way, we should encourage a student who wants to use algebra tiles, fraction bars, or counting bears to help them make sense of the math in their head.

Encouraging students to use manipulatives means they should be easily accessible. Many teachers have rulers, highlighters, and pencils placed where students can easily use them when needed. The same should be true of the manipulatives relevant to the current classwork. It is best if students do not have to make a special request for manipulatives, and if they do, it should be as streamlined as possible to avoid the possibility of any stigma associated with using manipulatives.

Virtual manipulatives can be just as effective as physical manipulatives, and they bring their own advantages and disadvantages. Students using virtual manipulatives are usually not limited by the number of manipulatives available. This allows students to model large or complicated tasks that require many manipulatives. Virtual manipulatives may offer additional features, such as automatically forming a zero pair when opposite integer chips are stacked. For some students, however, the physical objects may be easier to work with rather than operating a mouse or touchpad. Depending on availability and the needs of the individual student, virtual manipulatives can usually convey the same mathematical properties as their physical counterparts.

Developmental Progression

Manipulatives are a resource for making math more accessible. Teachers can use them to guide students through the Concrete-Representational-Abstract progression when developing new skills.

Concrete - At this stage, students use physical (or virtual) counters, manipulatives, money, or other objects to act out a problem or represent some aspect of the problem. This is an important stage in making sense of the mathematical relationships that are happening

Representational - Once students become more fluent with physical manipulatives, they typically progress to simplifying the concrete objects by sketching them or creating some other representation. Early in this phase, students may be literal in their representations, drawing integer chips, for example. Later, students become more efficient and might make dots on paper or draw tally marks to represent integer chips.

Abstract - This is the point when students have internalized the math represented by the manipulatives. They may still think about the manipulatives when working out problems, but they no longer feel the need to use them or draw them.

Each student will move through this progression at their own pace. Students may also move back and forth between the stages, particularly when dealing with new problem types. The teacher's goal is to allow students to move through these stages in order. It is not appropriate to teach abstract rules first, then ask students to model those rules with concrete items. That approach would make the manipulatives seem pointless or confusing to many students. Instead, teachers should continually move students closer to the abstract. Begin by exploring the manipulative very literally and slowly transition to the mathematical properties it represents.

One middle school class that stands out in my memory consisted exclusively of students who were two or more years behind their grade-level peers in their math ability. Every time I visited this class, however, students were creating posters of math work or having conversations about problems they were solving. One day when I visited class, students were solving simple integer addition and subtraction problems by modeling the questions with integer chips.

I sat with a student who exhibited developmental delays and watched as she modeled the same problems as her peers. She was not able to work as quickly, but she could accurately count out integer chips, match up zero pairs, and determine the solution. After working through a few problems, you could sense her fatigue and she lost interest in the integer chips and began doodling in her notebook.

The next time I visited class, most students were solving integer problems with number lines or a few lines of arithmetic on their paper. The student I had been sitting with had begun drawing integer chips instead of using the physical plastic disks. She would draw the correct amount of circles to represent the values in the problem and she carefully drew positive or negative symbols inside each circle. Then, like before, she would identify zero pairs and determine her solution.

Over the course of my visits, this student did not progress past the representational stage to the abstract stage. She likely would have done so with more time and some intentionally designed practice. But the level she reached was adequate that she could apply her understanding of integer operations to other problems such as comparing numbers, making changes, or even graphing in four quadrants. I am convinced that if her teacher had expected her to memorize a list of operational rules for adding and subtracting integers, it would have been more difficult for her to remember or to apply them in new settings.

Math manipulatives are a helpful tool for all students to build conceptual understanding. Students with IEPs typically benefit from intentionally designed practice using and applying manipulatives. Frustration with manipulatives can be a sign that students were not adequately instructed in their use or they were introduced after procedural rule-based instruction. With time and guidance, students will usually progress from physical (or virtual) manipulatives, to more efficient representations, and then to abstract thinking without the use of manipulatives. Each student will develop through these steps at their own pace, and some students may not reach all three stages. The underlying concepts behind using the manipulative, however, will benefit students regardless of their eventual level of fluency.

Part IV

After the Instruction

12 Assessment

This chapter on assessment is placed in the section of the book that describes tasks that happen after initial instruction. Effective assessment, however, is not so neatly contained. Evaluating students' understanding should be embedded within the entire lesson cycle. Teachers adjust their pacing by using informal monitoring of student conversations and the questions students are asking. Students reveal where they need additional support or review through brief checks for understanding. Many teachers use pre-assessments to determine what strategies to employ based on students' current strengths. In short, if teachers wait until after instruction to start thinking about assessment, it is much too late. Wherever assessment falls within the course of instruction, students with IEPs often require special consideration when it comes to the evaluation of their academic performance. Teachers have an ethical – and often legal – mandate to consider the student's unique needs when crafting and analyzing assessments.

Since different forms of assessment typically happen throughout the instructional cycle, this chapter will refer to some of the topics addressed elsewhere in this book. This section will summarize key components of assessment and how they impact students with IEPs.

Informal Assessment

Effective teachers constantly gather information about their students. Teaching is not a one-way broadcast of information. It is a two-way conversation between teachers and students. Teachers elicit information from their students through a variety of assessment tools, and this information helps shape instruction. A constant and informal system of assessment uses observations, questioning, or written checks for understanding to gauge students' academic progress.

Informal assessment is usually formative in nature. It happens while the instruction is still happening, and it helps teachers determine how to adjust their instruction. Based on what teachers learn through formative assessments, there are several general areas of instruction to adjust.

DOI: 10.4324/9781003346333-17

- Pacing - The speed of instruction will rarely suit all students. When instruction moves too quickly, students are left behind, exacerbating learning gaps. If the pace is too slow, students become bored and unengaged. When teachers determine that students need more time with a topic or are ready to move on, it is appropriate to find ways to adjust the pacing calendar. Students do not all learn at the same pace, so teachers often need to design some class time when students can practice different skills depending on their individual needs. The individual student needs will be even more diverse when students with IEPs are represented in the classroom. Teachers can maximize the impact of their classroom instructional time by deliberately planning in advance. Review any student information such as evaluation data, IEP goals, and information from the student's case manager. In extreme cases, teachers may also prioritize learning targets to use more class time for essential targets by taking time away from less significant concepts.
- Instructional approaches - With most topics in mathematics, there are several valid approaches to instruction. Teachers use their discretion to determine what order to present information, which connections to emphasize with other content, and the type and amount of practice to design. Formative assessment allows teachers to evaluate those decisions and adjust instruction when necessary. This can mean reordering learning targets, introducing different manipulatives or graphic organizers, or finding new ways to scaffold instruction. In some cases, Licensed Specialists in School Psychology who initially evaluate students for special education will also recommend effective instructional strategies.
- Differentiation - Students do not all learn the same way and they do not all bring the same background knowledge to class. Formative assessment can help teachers understand how to tailor instruction to the needs of specific students. Students do not all need to complete the same tasks or take identical assessments. Formative assessment helps teachers structure that differentiation. For students with IEPs, this differentiation can often align with SDI goals. This allows teachers to address IEP goals while also addressing math content needs.

The common methods of informal assessment in the math classroom include teacher observations of their students, verbal questions, and short written checks for understanding. These data sources are informal because they are brief, flexible, and sometimes subjective. They are still planned and intentional, and teachers often need to adjust these informal assessments for students with IEPs.

Teacher Observations

Teachers constantly monitor their students. They notice how quickly students are working, how engaged they are in the task, what approaches students use, whether students employ any manipulatives or graphic organizers, and what conversations are taking place. You can probably add several more items to this list. Each of these pieces of information can provide clues about how well students are understanding the math content and what they are ready to learn next. The observational clues may be different for neurodiverse students and students with IEPs. For example, we may listen for conversations that use appropriate math terminology with precision, but some students struggle with verbal expression, some students avoid sharing due to speech impairments, and other students are reserved due to anxiety. Peer conversation may not provide rich data for these groups of students.

Using observation to gauge student learning requires familiarity with our students. Particularly when working with students with IEPs, teacher observation notices any deviations from the classroom norm. Recognizing a particular student's normal level of performance allows teachers to observe when a student's work differs from their typical product. Teachers can notice, for example, whether specific students are working faster or slower than their normal pace. Teacher observations include listening to conversations, examining work-in-progress, and noticing general behaviors.

I can remember how hectic my first year of teaching was. I was trying to master the curriculum, manage behaviors, juggle paperwork, and make time to attend my own teacher certification classes. My math instruction was very procedural, and I typically spent each class period modeling a few sample problems and then trying to persuade my students to work on their independent practice. I logged countless miles rushing around the room as I redirected students to focus on their math work, wrote restroom passes, asked students to return to their seats, checked on students who didn't return from the restroom, and so on. I was learning on the go, and while things were getting better, I was usually exhausted.

One day, three or four weeks into the school year, I was debriefing the events of the day with my mentor teacher, and I told him I had experienced the smoothest class day so far. I described how my students that day were consistently on-task. I hadn't spent the period correcting behaviors and writing restroom passes. I had gotten to talk to students about their math work and actually felt like a teacher.

My mentor teacher's first reaction was to analyze the day's assignment. "I bet today's work was at just the right level," he theorized. "When students are engaged like that, the work is challenging enough that they aren't bored, but it's not so difficult that they can't do it."

I've always found it interesting that my mentor's thoughts immediately went to student readiness, pacing, and rigor. Of course, he recognized that my classroom management hadn't transformed overnight, so he looked toward other factors that influence student behaviors. His analysis sums up one of the ways that observation provides informal assessment. If your classroom procedures and routines are already in place, a change in student behaviors may indicate issues with the content. Some students act out when frustrated, overwhelmed, or bored. Any of those emotions could be a result of student learning gaps or content pacing that is too fast or too slow. Some students with IEPs have struggled with math for several years before they reach secondary school. In this situation, students sometimes cope by using behaviors to direct attention away from their academics. By observing student behaviors and looking for trends, teachers can tap into a rich source of informal assessment.

General classroom behaviors send a message about student performance. Changes in student engagement, math discourse, and on-task behavior can suggest that students are working in their comfort zone or that material is not appropriately aligned with student readiness. Similarly, student conversations and written work are revealing as well. The volume of student discourse can indicate how students have received a task. When students are given group work, there should be some conversation and discussion around their task. If the room – or a particular group – is silent, it may indicate they are unclear about the task or need help with group dynamics. As students reach the end of their work, the classroom volume usually drops momentarily, then increases as students find other (non-math) things to talk about. Teachers can listen for this drop in conversation as an indicator that students are ready to move on to something new.

Finally, looking at student work helps teachers identify specific misconceptions. In their book, *5 Practices for orchestrating productive mathematics discussions*, Smith & Stein (2016) recommend teachers anticipate areas in a task where students may encounter challenges. As teachers work through the task before class, they should approach the task with the same skills their students would use (don't use the quadratic formula if your students will use factoring). Then make note of common mistakes and what they might look like in student work. This gives the teacher a guide as they circulate around the classroom observing their students at work. By anticipating errors, it will be easier to recognize them on students' papers and help guide students back on track.

Questioning

Informal questioning can provide a quick method of assessing students in the math classroom. Teachers can implement a combination of both pre-planned questions that verify students are understanding the content and impromptu questions to probe student thinking and investigate possible misconceptions.

Pre-planned assessment questions are especially helpful with neurodiverse classrooms. Students do not work at the same pace, and it is important to recognize which students need more practice and which students are ready to move on. A quick verbal assessment helps keep the focus on student learning instead of focusing on completing the task. Once the student can demonstrate an understanding of today's learning goals, they can shift to the next assignment or spend time addressing learning gaps. Some examples of verbal assessment questions are listed here.

- How can you tell if the data listed in a two-column table has a positive or negative correlation?
- What are some examples of continuous and discrete data?
- How can you calculate the unit price for an item in the grocery store?

If students can't answer the question about the day's work, they may need additional practice or a conversation about the content.

Teachers can also craft questions on-the-fly to learn more about student thinking. Often student work does not reveal everything we want to know as teachers. A few questions can explore student understanding. Figure 12.1 shows an example of student work and suggests some follow-up questions to determine how well the student understands the concept of slope.

Sometimes we need more information than we can find in student work, and it is important not to make assumptions when a student does not include their written work on their paper. Students may have communication problems such as autism spectrum disorder or challenges with written expression. Students may struggle with anxiety and may need encouragement to share the rough draft of their math work. In all these cases, verbal questioning may provide an alternative information source. Chapter 10 explores the use of

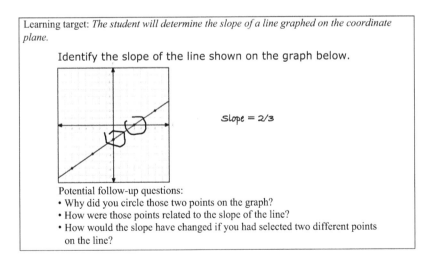

Learning target: *The student will determine the slope of a line graphed on the coordinate plane.*

Identify the slope of the line shown on the graph below.

Slope = 2/3

Potential follow-up questions:
- Why did you circle those two points on the graph?
- How were those points related to the slope of the line?
- How would the slope have changed if you had selected two different points on the line?

Figure 12.1 This student's paper does not show how they arrived at the answer. Some follow-up questions would be appropriate to determine what the student truly understands about the concept of slope.

assessing questions more in-depth as well as reminders about adjusting questions to meet the needs of neurodiverse students.

Written Checks for Understanding

Another tool for informally gauging student progress is short, written checks for understanding. Many teachers incorporate these into exit tickets at the end of class or warm-up tasks at the beginning of class. These checks are still formative assessments because they happen before the instruction is completed and they provide information so the teacher can adjust classwork to respond to student needs. They offer some advantages over verbal questioning. Written checks create an efficient way for all students to respond. The written record allows the teacher to analyze each student's response and plan differentiated groupings or other interventions based on the results.

By including a range of questions, teachers can learn a significant amount of information from a single check for understanding. Designing a collection of low-rigor and high-rigor questions allows each student to demonstrate their current level of understanding. This sample list of questions demonstrates how a set of questions can progressively increase in challenge.

- What is the area of a triangle with a base of 3 feet and a height of 8 feet?
- A triangle has a base of 5 inches and an area of 35 square inches. What is the triangle's height?
- Draw and label the dimensions of three different triangles, each with an area of 24 square inches.

The final question is intended to be accessible to all students while offering an open-ended element that allows students to challenge themselves in their responses. This design lets teachers gather information on each student regardless of their current level of readiness.

Since each student has unique strengths and needs, not all informal data sources are effective for all students. Written checks for understanding may not reveal information about students who struggle with written expression. Questioning will look different when working with students who struggle with verbal expression or require increased processing time. Implementing a wide range of informal assessments in the classroom allows teachers to use alternative data sources when necessary. Teachers may find they have to piece together many small snippets of information to create a full picture of a student's academic progress.

Some students with IEPs do not communicate as freely as their peers. This may be a feature of their neurodiversity. Students may struggle with verbal expression or communication in general, making it difficult to ask for help when it is needed. Issues with communication or social connections will make it challenging for teachers to gather informal information from student discourse. It can be difficult to determine if a student is not joining in the classroom discussion because they are uncomfortable with the math content or because of personal characteristics. Other students may not engage with their peers because of anxiety due to a lack of prior success in math class, speech issues, language development, or other issues that affect adolescent learners. Similarly, if students require additional processing time or deal with Specific Learning Disabilities in reading, teachers may replace written checks for understanding with verbal questions.

Formal Assessment

Regular quizzes and tests comprise the more formal component of classroom assessment. These are usually more summative in nature because they take place after instruction to measure what students have learned and retained. Teachers can still help struggling students continue developing the skills covered in these tests and quizzes, but their purpose is different from the informal assessment which is used to adjust instruction.

Quality assessments can serve as a guide for instruction as it provides a target for teachers as they are designing classwork. When teachers begin their planning by crafting assessments, they know exactly the level of rigor their students must achieve. Generally, planning would proceed in this order:

1 Choose learning targets - Using curriculum documents – including the scope and sequence – teachers should identify exactly what skills and knowledge students need to develop. This includes determining the level of rigor students must achieve.
2 Write assessment - Next, teachers should write the assessments they will use to determine whether students have mastered these learning targets. Writing the assessments before instruction begins helps provide a target for in-class learning and guarantees that teachers do not deviate from the learning goals during or after instruction. By writing the assessment before the teaching happens, teachers are committing to the standard they expect their students to achieve. Teachers should ensure at this point that the rigor of their assessment meets the expectations of the learning targets.
3 Modify and accommodate assessment - Any assessment accommodations and modifications described in a student's IEP are a legal mandate. In addition to developing alternate versions of assessments, teachers should begin planning how they will teach students to use any allowable supplemental aids, manipulatives, or graphic organizers.
4 Design instruction - After these steps are completed, it is time to design instruction that will address the learning targets and prepare students for success on the assessments. The previously-designed assessments should

influence the rigor of the instruction. For example, will problems include fractions, decimals, or negative numbers? How many steps will students have to perform? Will students calculate or explain?

As indicated in these steps, formal assessments should be designed prior to designing classroom instruction. This helps ensure that instruction is aligned with the quizzes and tests. After drafting the assessment, it is important to adjust assessments to meet the needs of diverse learners in the classroom. In many circumstances, it is not necessary for all students to take the same test. Some students may take a shorter version of the test, a version with accommodated questions, or in some cases a test over slightly different content.

When creating accommodated assessments, read through the test looking for obstacles that will inhibit student performance, and consider which of those obstacles can be removed.

- Check for vocabulary that is not related to the math content that may confuse some students.
- Consider whether some problems use context or experiences that are not common to all class members.
- Look for opportunities to remove extraneous calculations that are not related to the intent of the question.

Examine the example problems in Table 12.1 and keep track of obstacles that could be removed without impacting the math content.

Table 12.1 These sample problems each contain potential obstacles that are not related to the math content. When teachers accommodate or modify assessments, they should consider ways to remove obstacles like these

Learning Target: The student will use proportional reasoning to solve problems using scale.
 1 On a particular map, a distance of 15 blocks is represented by a distance of 6 cm. On the same map, what distance would represent a distance of 24 blocks?

Learning Target: The student will solve problems using multiplication and division or rational numbers.
 2 Dylan is using a recipe to make cookies. The recipe requires 3½ cups of flour for each batch of cookies. If Dylan wants to make 1.5 batches of cookies, how much flour will Dylan need?

Learning Target: The student will use the rate of change to solve problems involving linear relationships.
 3 A shipping company charges a pickup fee plus a delivery fee that depends on the weight of the package being shipped. A 10-pound package costs $20 to ship, and a 20-pound package costs $35 to ship. How much would it cost to ship a 22-pound package that is 12 inches wide?

In question 1, the word "blocks" is used in a way that may be unfamiliar to some students. This could be replaced with kilometers or miles without losing any of the math content. Some students may benefit from a diagram illustrating this question. The cooking context in question 2 may not be familiar to all students. Some students may perform better on this question if it uses a situation they can connect with. Question 3 includes a distracting detail about the dimensions of the 22-pound package that could be removed. This problem could also benefit from adding a table to organize information. The appropriateness of these accommodations depends on the individual student.

Chapter 7 explores accommodations and modifications in greater detail, and Table 12.2 summarizes some of the high-impact accommodations to consider when creating a math test.

Table 12.2 These are common accommodations for tests in a math class. Each accommodation should be applied according to individual student needs

Accommodation	Rationale
Rephrase a problem to begin and end with the question.	For students who struggle with reading skills or have limited attention, this strategy provides a guide for students to help them know what information they need as they read the question.
Chunking large blocks of text.	For students with language, reading, or attention issues, this breaks the information into digestible pieces helping students break down the action of the problem.
Remove extraneous information.	For students who need additional processing time or struggle with math reasoning, this helps them focus on the pertinent match by removing distractions.
Simplify vocabulary.	For students with language, reading, attention, or processing issues, this unfamiliar vocabulary is an unnecessary obstacle.
Insert formulas or graphic organizers.	For students who struggle with math reasoning, math calculation, short-term memory, or attention issues, this helps organize information and make sense of the question while still expecting students to perform the same calculations as their peers.
Include or label diagrams.	For students with math reasoning or reading difficulties, this supplements the text of a problem by illustrating the context of the problem.

Keep in mind that accommodations and modifications should be aligned with the needs of the individual student. Sometimes it will be necessary to make multiple accommodated versions of a test for one class. Teachers should also discuss accommodations with students regularly to make sure the accommodations are effective and to consider removing supports over time.

Reference

Smith, M. S., & Stein, M. K. (2016). *5 Practices for orchestrating productive mathematics discussions*. The National Council of Teachers of Mathematics.

13 Testing Accommodations

When I was in middle school, my handwriting was usually indecipherable. However, one of my algebra classmates, Scott, wrote in immaculate script. Each letter was perfectly formed, their heights were identical, and his notes were a thing of beauty.

And it took him forever to write anything down.

Scott wrote carefully, clearly, and painfully slowly. He often borrowed my notes so he could finish writing what he missed because the teacher moved on before Scott could finish writing everything down. Scott was also always the last one to finish his test. He was incapable of writing faster, and sometimes that slow pace hurt his grade. Scott knew his math and had no problems with algebra, but he rarely finished an entire test before class time was over. He usually did not earn any credit for the last two or three questions on any exam, because he just hadn't made it that far before the teacher insisted on collecting his test so he wouldn't be late for his next class.

For Scott, his test scores were not a reflection of what he knew about algebra. They were a reflection of what he could communicate through writing during an arbitrarily determined time limit of 48 minutes.

Sometimes a test does not assess what we think it is assessing.

Teachers always want to be aware of what their classroom tests are really evaluating. If tests are a tool for measuring where students are now and what skills they are ready to develop next, that tool is only effective if the test is aligned with the teaching standards. It would not have been helpful to place my friend Scott in a math intervention group – even though his test papers seemed to show he could not even attempt some of the algebra problems.

Our classrooms are filled with a diverse collection of students, and it is impossible to evaluate all those students with a single test administered in a uniform way. Chapter 2 of this book describes several cognitive abilities. Often students will need to draw on multiple cognitive abilities to solve a single test question. For students who struggle in one or more of those cognitive abilities, the test questions pose an additional set of challenges that are not always related to the math content. Adjusting test questions for a

DOI: 10.4324/9781003346333-18

specific student based on their specific needs can happen through *modification* or *accommodation*.

The more intense type of test adjustment, *modification*, happens when educators adjust a test so that it addresses different knowledge or skills or at a lower level of rigor. A modified test should only be used if a student is receiving a different curriculum from their peers. The details on test modification should be outlined in the student's IEP, describing what content should be modified and what modifications should be implemented. A sample test item and some modifications are provided in Figure 13.1. A modified test might address the same skill as the original test but at a different level of rigor. Perhaps the original test asked students to graph linear inequalities written in standard form, but the modified test provided the inequalities in slope-intercept form. Modifications might include testing a different skill that is still within the vertical alignment. For example, if the original test assesses students' ability to graph the solutions to a system of two-variable inequalities, a modified test might ask a student to graph a system of equations. This is a related, necessary skill, but it is a different skill from the original test.

By contrast, adjusting a test so that the question truly evaluates the intended content – and not a separate cognitive ability – is called *accommodation*. When teachers accommodate a test, their goal is to make the test accessible to specific

(a)   (b)   (c)

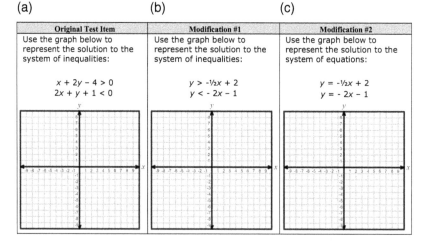

Original Test Item	Modification #1	Modification #2
Use the graph below to represent the solution to the system of inequalities:	Use the graph below to represent the solution to the system of inequalities:	Use the graph below to represent the solution to the system of equations:
$x + 2y - 4 > 0$ $2x + y + 1 < 0$	$y > -\frac{1}{2}x + 2$ $y < -2x - 1$	$y = -\frac{1}{2}x + 2$ $y = -2x - 1$

Figure 13.1 The original question was intended to assess students' ability to represent a system of two-variable inequalities graphically. Modification #1 tests the skill at a different level of rigor by providing the inequalities in slope-intercept form. Modification #2 tests a different skill within the vertical alignment by asking students to graph a system of equations. Both modifications represent a separate curriculum from the original and should only be used in accordance with the specific student's IEP.

students *while still addressing the original content knowledge and skills at the original level of rigor.* The best testing accommodations do not make a test easier than the original test and they do not test different skills than the original test. They do, however, remove obstacles that prevent some students from demonstrating their content knowledge.

To understand what non-curricular obstacles are present in a test, it is helpful to list all the skills a student will use to correctly solve the problems. Sometimes a teacher colleague can provide a fresh set of eyes and help notice facets of a question that teachers may overlook. Try this activity. Read through the problems in Figure 13.2, and list all the skills students will need when solving the problem.

In the shadow problem, students must understand the characteristics of similar figures, identify corresponding parts of similar figures, generate a proportion representing the relationship between the dimensions of two similar figures, and solve a proportion to calculate a missing value. Visually, students must recognize the smaller similar triangle embedded within the larger triangle. Additionally, students must translate between the verbal problem and the diagram so they can apply arithmetic to find some missing measurements. (Students must determine that the smaller similar triangle has a base of 10 yards.) There is also some vocabulary that may be unfamiliar to some students, particularly Emergent Bilingual students, and students will benefit from prior experience with similar triangles formed by shadows.

There is a considerable amount of knowledge students need that is not directly related to similar figures and proportional relationships. However, there are

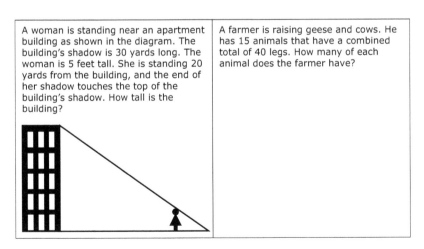

Figure 13.2 List the knowledge and skills students must use to successfully solve each of these problems. Consider which of those skills are obstacles that prevent students from demonstrating their math understanding.

challenges directly related to cognitive abilities as well. Students need to rely on their visual processing skills to notice the similar triangles in the diagram and match the dimensions from the problem to their appropriate locations in the figure. Unless students have worked with a similar problem before, they are likely to need fluid reasoning skills to apply their knowledge to a new problem type. For students with limited working memory, using the numbers in the problem to calculate new measurements may be a struggle that will require carefully organizing the information provided. For some students, these obstacles may be significant enough that teachers should adjust the problem so that it still tests a student's ability to find the missing dimension in a pair of similar figures, but with fewer auxiliary skills.

The geese-and-cow problem is a traditional system of equations problem where we expect students to write equations to represent the information in the problem. Students will need to define variables and use the relationships between those variables to write equations. Students will then solve that system of equations, and they have a few different ways to do that. However, students may also be distracted by the context of the problem, or students with specific learning disabilities in reading may struggle to make sense of the problem as written.

However, students can successfully solve this problem without applying their knowledge of systems of equations. Fifth-grade students have the skills necessary to create a table showing the number of legs different collections of animals will have (see Table 13.1). This suggests the geese-and-cow problem may not be a good indicator of whether students can write and solve systems of two-variable equations.

Table 13.1 Students can create an organized table to solve the "Geese and Cows" problem presented in Figure 13.2. Because of this alternate approach, this problem may not be an effective question for measuring students' ability to create and solve a system of equations

Number of Geese	Number of Cows	Number of Legs
0	15	60
1	14	58
2	13	56
3	12	54
4	11	52
5	10	50
6	9	48
7	8	46
8	7	44
9	6	42
10	5	40

Teachers work to design tests aligned with the instructional standards. When teachers have an accurate picture of what students know and where they are still struggling, it effectively informs future instruction. This means finding (or creating) questions that address the intended knowledge and skills, and it means eliminating the additional obstacles some students will face with particular test questions.

High-Impact Testing Accommodations for Math

Secondary mathematics is more than arithmetic. It is important for students to develop their skills as problem solvers, communicators, and critical thinkers. Students should be able to apply their math knowledge to the world around them. When it comes to accommodating math tests, the challenge is to make the question accessible without removing the reasoning and problem-solving that students need to develop. Here we explore several suggestions for math test accommodations that attempt to balance accessibility with rigor.

Rewording and Chunking

As students move from elementary to secondary school, the focus of math is less on one-step arithmetic and more on multi-step problem solving and application of skills. This often results in wordy problems that many students find intimidating. Figure 13.3 shows how a large block of text can be broken up into smaller chunks to help students make sense of the problem without changing its meaning or level of rigor.

This approach is often appropriate for students with an SLD in any area of reading, difficulties in visual processing or working memory, language issues

Original Test Item	Accommodated Test Item
Max and Chris are collecting food for a canned food drive. Max started with 12 cans of food and is collecting 3 cans each day. Chris began with 8 cans of food and collects 5 cans of food each day. On which day will both Max and Chris have the same number of cans of food?	A club at school is getting cans of food. • Max started with 12 cans of food • Max gets 3 more cans each day • Chris started with 8 cans of food • Chris gets 5 more cans each day When will both Max and Chris have the same number of cans of food?

Figure 13.3 The original problem is one large block of text which can create an obstacle for students with visual, language, or attention issues. The revised question allows students to gather information in smaller chunks.

(including Emergent Bilingual students), and students with ADHD who have trouble focusing on long portions of text. This strategy can include:

- Chunking or bulleting information to help students process small segments of information
- Rewording non-content vocabulary to help students understand the meaning of the problem
- Adding white space so that the block of text is not overwhelming

Eliminating Distracting Information

Math word problems are notorious for including distracting information that students do not need to use in finding the solution. It is a very valuable skill for students to distinguish between useful facts and extraneous details. If students are not ready to make that distinction, however, distracting information can make it difficult for teachers to determine what math knowledge and skills students have mastered. Teachers should help students determine what information is useful, but while students are still practicing that skill, it can be helpful to eliminate extra information from test items as shown in Figure 13.4.

Original Test Item	Accommodated Test Item
A local packing plant ships items across the entire state, sending out hundreds of boxes each day. The plant charges its customers based on the number of packages they ship and the volume of the packages. The largest packages the company ships measure more than 20 cubic feet. The plant uses the formula: $c = b\,(3 + v)$ to determine c, how much to charge their customers. In this formula, b represents the number of packages and v represents the volume of each package, measured in cubic feet. If the plant ships 25 packages that each measure 8.5 cubic feet, how much should they charge their customer?	A business ships boxes and customers pay based on the number of boxes and their volume. The formula: $c = b\,(3 + v)$ calculates c, the amount customers will pay. In this formula, b represents the number of boxes and v represents their volume, measured in cubic feet. If the business ships 25 boxes that each measure 8.5 cubic feet, how much will the customer pay?

Figure 13.4 In this example, extra details have been removed and the language has been simplified. Notice the word "plant" has been replaced with "business" so students are not distracted by the secondary definition of the original word. Removing the distracting details helps the student focus on the important information they need and it allows teachers to get a true indication of what skills students have mastered.

Original Test Item	Accommodated Test Item
A 12-foot ladder is leaning against the outside wall of a building. The base of the ladder is 6 feet away from the building. How high up the building does the ladder reach?	A 12-foot ladder is leaning against the outside wall of a building as shown in the diagram. The base of the ladder is 6 feet away from the building. How high up the building does the ladder reach?

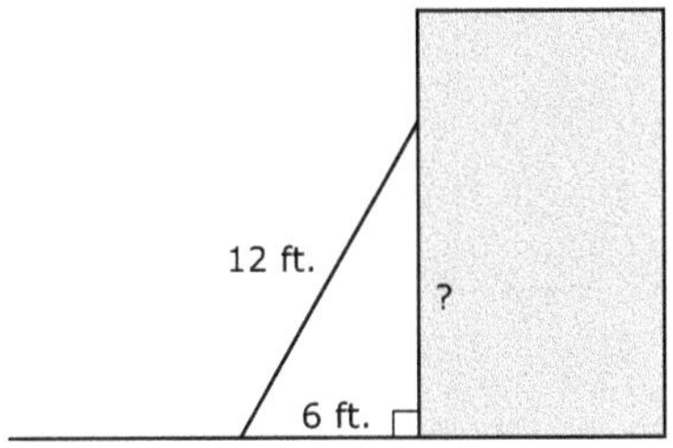

Figure 13.5 Adding a diagram to this problem organizes the information in the problem for students.

This is a support that teachers should feather over time, but it can be especially helpful for students with SLDs in reading, Emergent Bilingual students, and students with attention issues.

Inserting Diagrams

Adding figures or diagrams to a math problem can make everything clearer. Depending on the goal of the test item, teachers can adjust the amount of detail in the diagram and decide whether or not the diagram is pre-labeled with information from the text. This is also an opportunity to teach students to become more independent as teachers can initially provide detailed diagrams, then feather the support as students can generate more and more information on their own. Figure 13.5 shows how a Pythagorean Theorem question still asks students to determine the length of a missing dimension on a right triangle, but the support of a diagram makes the question more accessible.

This support is appropriate for students with SLDs in reading or students who struggle to organize information due to attention issues. Providing a diagram may be helpful for some students who have issues with visual processing, but that may depend on the individual student.

Providing Graphic Organizers and/or Formulas

Often students know a significant amount of math, but they are not sure how or when to apply it. Graphic organizers like the one shown in Figure 13.6 can help

Original Test Item	Accommodated Test Item		
The ratio of cars to trucks at a local car dealership is 5 to 2. If there are 350 vehicles at the dealership, how many trucks are there?	The ratio of cars to trucks at a local car dealership is 5 to 2. If there are 350 vehicles at the dealership, how many trucks are there?		
		Ratio	Dealership
	Cars	5	
	Trucks	2	
	Total		350

Figure 13.6 Inserting this table in this problem shows students how to organize this information and suggests strategies they can use to continue working out the problem.

students make sense of the information they are using to solve a problem and can help students estimate answers or understand what math they are using.

For students who struggle with working memory, it can also be helpful to provide the formulas they will use to solve a problem adjacent to the question. This prevents students from having to move between a test and a reference page.

Begin and End with the Question

Students practice academic reading in most of their classes, and they learn several reading strategies to help them understand the text they read. Math problems, however, usually follow a different structure from writing in other subject areas. In most content areas, a reading passage starts with a main idea, follows with supporting information, and ends with a conclusion that summarizes the key points of the passage. Math problems are almost written in a reversed structure. Math passages begin with supporting details, include some extraneous information, then conclude with the main idea: the question or purpose of the entire problem. Table 13.2 compares these two structures side-by-side.

Table 13.2 The passages that students read in a math class are often written in a different format from the passages students read in other content areas. This makes it difficult for students to apply their reading strategies to the problems they read in their math class

Typical Non-Math Reading Passage	Typical Math Reading Passage
• Main Idea or Topic Statement	• Supporting Details
• Supporting Details	• Irrelevant information
• Conclusion or Summary	• Main Idea (the *question*)

Original Test Item	Accommodated Test Item
Dylan planted a tree in their backyard and measured its height each year. The table below shows how tall the tree was each year.	How tall will Dylan's tree be in year 8? Dylan planted a tree in their backyard and measured its height each year. The table below shows how tall the tree was each year.

Original Test Item table:

Year	Height (ft.)
1	5.5
2	7
3	8.5
4	10

Based on the data in the table, predict how tall Dylan's tree will be in year 8.

Accommodated Test Item table:

Year	Height (ft.)
1	5.5
2	7
3	8.5
4	10

Based on the data in the table, predict how tall Dylan's tree will be in year 8.

Figure 13.7 By beginning and ending with the question students are asked to solve, the teacher provides a guide for students as they read the remainder of the problem and determine which details are useful and which are distracting.

This inverted writing structure can confuse students who try to apply reading strategies they have learned in their other classes. It also means students have to read and recall the details of the entire problem before they find out how they will use the information when they get to the end of the passage. Since students don't know yet what the question is asking, they cannot determine which information is important and which information is extraneous. This can be a challenge for students with limited working memory as well as students with SLDs in reading.

One simple approach to support students is writing problems so that they begin and end with the question. By starting with the question, students now have a guide. This provides a framework for students to use as they read the rest of the problem, considering what information they will need and how they will apply it. Figure 13.7 shows what this might look like.

Students can be taught to apply this strategy on their own when they are ready to become more independent. Students might read a problem twice – one time to identify the question and a second time to identify key details. Students may be taught to highlight the question, then analyze the rest of the text.

Writing in the Second Person

Many teachers rewrite word problems to include their students' names. This can help students form a connection to a problem. Students notice their names and find the problems more interesting. When students recognize themselves or a

Original Test Item	Accommodated Test Item
Taylor started working at a local ice cream shop. They earn $10.50 per hour for serving ice cream and cleaning the shop. If Taylor worked 15 hours last week, how many more hours do they need to work to earn a total of at least $200?	You started working at a local ice cream shop. You earn $10.50 per hour for serving ice cream and cleaning the shop. If you worked 15 hours last week, how many more hours do you need to work to earn a total of at least $200?

Figure 13.8 Replacing a name in a math problem with the second-person "you" can make students feel more connected to the problem and help them engage with the question.

peer in a problem, they may become more engaged and invested in the problem (Davis-Dorsey 1991). A simple way to simulate this effect is to rewrite work problems in the second person, placing "you" in the problem. This shift in perspective can increase students' reading comprehension as they mentally picture the action of the problem. This is a very minor adjustment as shown in Figure 13.8, and it can engage students who have trouble focusing without changing the content of the problem or its level or rigor.

Oral Administration

Oral administration of tests is often associated with reading SLDs such as reading comprehension. Simply reading test questions aloud (or providing access to an audio recording of the test or text-to-speech technology) may benefit some students. If teachers are planning to implement this approach with secondary students, it is important to acclimate students to the accommodation and create an environment where students are comfortable having a test read to them. There can be some stigma associated with having a test read aloud while the student is in the same room as peers. Conversations between the teacher and the individual students will help determine if this form of oral administration will be helpful.

Another approach is a one-on-one oral assessment of the student. Some students struggle with tests not because of any math-related issues, but because of anxiety or trouble communicating. Students with an SLD in written expression may not be able to effectively respond to open-ended questions. Other students may *freeze-up* when asked to perform on a test. Meeting with the student and assessing their content knowledge through a teacher-student conference may address either of these situations. This approach can be time-consuming, so it is not a solution for all cases. This approach does allow a teacher to individualize the experience and truly understand what a student knows.

Of course, the accommodations illustrated in this chapter can be combined in different ways according to the individual student's needs. With modifications and accommodations, the long-term goal is to help students become more indepen-dent. Though some students may never outgrow these supports, educators can still facilitate students' development. It is important not to over-support students. Teachers will need to monitor students' work and talk to students regularly about what scaffolds are still necessary and what supports students have outgrown. This work should, of course, also be documented and used to update IEP documents.

Reference

Davis-Dorsey, Ross, S. M., & Morrison, G. R. (1991). The role of rewording and context personalization in the solving of mathematical word problems. *Journal of Educational Psychology, 83*(1), 61–68. 10.1037/0022-0663.83.1.61

14   Data Analysis

Assessments help teachers and students look backward to measure learning growth, they describe the present level of achievement, and they can look ahead to where classroom instruction is ready to take students next. Using assessments to look forward requires teachers to collect rich data from students and analyze that data looking for trends and opportunities for growth. Test grades do not have to be viewed as the end of instruction and learning, but rather as a checkpoint along a path and an opportunity to correct the course. This chapter will explore helpful strategies for analyzing assessment data as well as using assessments to engage students in their learning.

Student Self-Analysis

Students can overemphasize test scores as the primary measure of learning. As teachers, we understand it is impossible to describe a person with a single score or assessment. We can, however, help students to better understand how their test performance fits into the bigger picture of their journey as a learner. Teachers can clearly describe to students which knowledge and skills a particular test addressed – and did not address. Since assessments may not accurately measure the abilities of students with IEPs, it is even more important to help students in this population interpret the meaning of their test scores and how we can use them to plan future learning.

To engage students in analyzing their own assessment data, teachers should begin with student-friendly learning targets. Students should clearly understand what skills the assessment covers. This may mean translating pedagogical language into statements that are meaningful to students. Table 14.1 contains examples of learning targets originally written in the technical language common to curriculum documents, then modified into language that is clearer for students. This allows learners to better track their own progress in relation to learning goals.

Next, students need an efficient way to match those student-friendly targets to the work they performed on the assessment. A classroom unit test may include

DOI: 10.4324/9781003346333-19

Table 14.1 Learning targets written in student-friendly language help students monitor their own academic progress

Original Learning Target	Student-Friendly Target
The student will compare and order rational numbers using a number line.	The student will place fractions, decimals, and percents correctly on a number line.
The student will identify key features of quadratic functions on the coordinate graph.	The student will locate the vertex, zeros, and line of symmetry on the graph of a quadratic function.
The student will solve problems using the Pythagorean Theorem and its converse.	The student will use the Pythagorean Theorem to calculate the length of a side of a right triangle and to determine whether a triangle contains a right angle.

Table 14.2 Breaking down test scores according to specific learning standards helps students understand the test results and target their next steps

Traditional Assessment Summary	Descriptive Assessment Summary
Unit Test: Quadratic Functions • 80% Correct	Unit Test: Quadratic Functions • Graphing Quadratic Functions from an Equation: 100% • Identifying Vertex and Line of Symmetry: 90% • Identifying zeros: 50%

three or four learning targets. Traditionally, math students have received a single summary score for an assessment. Many students do not analyze their work much further than reading that single grade at the top of their test papers. It can be much more informative to break down a test score according to the skills that were assessed and help students identify their performance on each skill. Table 14.2 contrasts the traditional summary test score with a more descriptive approach that helps students understand exactly where their current strengths and weaknesses lie.

This clear breakdown of learning targets will help students gauge their mastery by analyzing multiple sources of data. When students understand which skill or concept the assessment addressed, they can more easily find classwork or notes on the same topic. Students can compare their performance across multiple assignments and assessments, measuring growth and determining whether they have achieved a level of mastery they are satisfied with. Multiple data points are particularly helpful when working with students who struggle with retention or attention. Measuring mastery over time gives a truer picture of student learning than a single snapshot taken shortly after instruction was delivered.

Table 14.3 Students can track their own learning progress over time with a table like this one. In this example, even though the student is still working on the second learning target, they can observe the growth in their skill since the first assignment on this content

Learning Target	Assignment 1	Assignment 2	Assignment 3	Assessment	Retest
I can identify the slope from a table	67	82	80	85	
I can use an equation to complete a table	55	67		67	75

Particularly for students with IEPs, it can be encouraging to measure progress over time instead of focusing on snapshots of student mastery. If students can see their test performance broken down by learning target, they can also track their performance on that learning target over the course of several assignments and assessments. Table 14.3 shows an example of a tracking document students can use to monitor their performance and better understand what skills they are still working on and which ones they have mastered. Struggling students can see growth, even in areas they are still working to improve.

When students can understand their test performance broken down by learning target, it gives them clearer guidance as they respond to assessment data. Students can see where their strengths are and what skills still need their attention. If teachers tailor reteach activities and retests to target those areas of student need, it can increase student buy-in. When students understand they are focusing on the specific skills they need to sharpen, they feel their prior performance has been honored. When teachers allow students to retake specific portions of a test – instead of working through the entire assessment – it respects the student's demonstration of learning and acknowledges the value of the student's past work. This does not mean that students should not revisit past content. Spaced practice over prior skills helps solidify learning and is a valuable practice to employ with students with IEPs.

Finally, engaging students in the analysis of their own work often means providing flexibility for students to set their own learning goals. Teachers, curriculum documents, and professional learning communities should determine which learning objectives to prioritize. Students, however, should be afforded the freedom to set their own academic goals when appropriate. Teachers and students can work together to determine timelines or levels of mastery that still address essential learning while giving students ownership of their own learning.

The Value of Student Work Samples

Any analysis is only as good as the data. Most math teachers can remember a time they have examined a student's test trying to understand how the student arrived at their answers. This is why many teachers stress the importance of students showing their work. Student work leaves an evidence trail that makes student thinking visible.

If the only data teachers have are multiple-choice test responses, they will be limited in the types of data analysis they can perform. If a student chose the right answer, the teacher always has to consider the possibility that the student chose the correct response by chance and not through any application of skill. Similarly, when a student chooses the wrong answer, it can be difficult to tell how deep the student's misconception lies. Looking only at the answers to a multiple-choice test, teachers cannot easily discriminate between a small arithmetic mistake and a major misunderstanding of the concept.

When teachers examine student work, however, it provides new levels of information. There is a balance between the convenience of multiple-choice testing and the detail of written exams or oral questioning. But the closer teachers can get to artifacts of student thinking, the better. Sometimes students can write their calculations or create diagrams. Other times teachers may ask students a few questions about how they arrived at an answer.

When teachers are working together with grade-level teams, it can be helpful to share a few samples of student work. Other teachers can provide objective observations that offer new insights into student work. Student work samples from different classes also lend themselves to broad themes. Teachers can determine if all students are struggling with similar issues or if some teachers are more effectively addressing misconceptions. As teachers review student work, they should try to answer two questions:

- What does this student know?
- What is this student ready to learn next?

The first question helps teachers focus on students' strengths and current abilities. It is easy to be frustrated by students' learning gaps. It can be tempting to overlook what students already know and begin reviewing too many fundamental skills. A recent study observed that almost 75% of classroom assignments are below grade level (TNTP 2018). This represents almost four days out of every school week. This environment makes it almost impossible for students to master current grade-level material. Teachers have a responsibility to address essential gaps in learning, but they are also responsible for providing targeted support. Most of the time, the entire classroom of students does not exhibit the same gap, so a class-wide review assignment over last year's material is usually not appropriate. Instead, gap-filling tasks should be designed for specific skills and assigned to the specific students who need the support. By asking themselves "What does this student know?" teachers are acknowledging what prior knowledge specific students will not need to review. This frees up time to build new skills.

Those new skills are the subject of the second question: "What is this student ready to learn next?" Based on the student's current performance, teachers can identify what missing component will best benefit the student's learning. If a student can calculate the slope of a line, maybe it is time to practice writing equations in slope-intercept form. If a student can calculate simple probabilities, they may be ready to make predictions of simple events.

If teachers find they struggle to answer these questions based on student data, then it should prompt them to look for new data sources. It is more difficult to answer these questions based on multiple-choice data, so teachers may need to collect student work or have brief conversations with students. Understanding what information the data will provide will help teachers understand how to write assessments in order to collect the information they will need.

Identifying Themes

Each student in today's math classroom has a different constellation of skills, abilities, interests, and learning gaps. It is impractical to create fully individualized assignments each day for these individual learners. Teachers can, however, create tailored learning experiences for groups of students. If these student groups are flexible enough, each student can receive the instruction they need when they are ready for it.

As teachers look at assessment data, they should try to identify themes across the information. The most basic sorting comes from identifying which students missed specific questions (e.g., this list of students missed question #4). If a cluster of assessment questions addresses a specific learning target, it may be more valuable to sort students according to which learning targets are mastered. A teacher may notice that even though a student missed question #4, their work on the rest of the test shows that the student still mastered the skill that question addressed. If a classroom assessment covers two or three learning targets, teachers can generate a list of students who still need to work on each target. There is likely to be some overlap between the lists as certain students may need help with two targets or all three.

The next step is to try to determine what specific obstacles students are experiencing with each learning target. Teachers will often take some student papers and begin looking for trends. They can see if students are struggling to understand which operation(s) to use, making arithmetic mistakes, misidentifying information from the problem, or struggling in other areas. It may not be necessary to look at all student papers at this point. A few samples of work can be adequate to determine what areas need to be addressed.

After these steps, teachers should have identified a few specific misunderstandings for each learning target. They now need to sort students into groups according to these categories. Teachers can do the sorting themselves by examining each test paper and looking for specific signs in student answers or work. Alternatively, teachers can have students sort themselves into these groups. If teachers can describe each deficit in student-friendly language, students can use their test papers to determine where they need help. Teachers can guide students through this process. For example, we might hear a teacher tell the class:

> "Look at the volume questions on your test. If you missed two or more questions and you weren't sure which formula to use, you'll be in the blue group today. If you missed two or more questions and you didn't know how to multiply the mixed numbers in those problems, you'll be in the green group."

This involves students in their own remediation and encourages them to think about their current level of understanding. In the example above, there may be students in class that do not know which volume formula to use and do not know how to multiply mixed numbers. Students can decide for themselves which group will be more beneficial. They may choose the group they believe they can experience more success in or the group they feel they have the greatest need for.

Planning for data analysis helps teachers become better assessment writers as they consider what data they need about their students. Data analysis is also a vital step in planning and executing meaningful instructional interventions. If teachers are going to intentionally address student misconceptions and learning gaps, it is important to have detailed and specific information about current ability. Teachers may need to collect multiple data points to form an accurate picture when working with students with IEPs, but forming a more complete picture of student ability will ultimately benefit future instruction.

Many teachers have experienced a time when it seems that the entire class of students is struggling to the point that it feels necessary to start from the beginning. This is where data analysis helps us resist the urge to think, "no one gets it, no one gets any of it." Each student is unique, and by taking time to review the data, we start to notice which specific students are struggling and recognize the features of their specific struggles. The next chapter describes how teachers respond after first-time instruction, but data analysis lays the essential groundwork before teachers can begin addressing the needs of specific groups of students.

Reference

TNTP. (2018). (rep.). The Opportunity Myth. Retrieved from https://tntp.org/publications/view/student-experiences/the-opportunity-myth

15   Intervention

When we are sick, we don't go to the doctor for a diagnosis. We go to the doctor for a treatment plan. Sure, it's important to know why we don't feel well, but what we are really interested in are the steps to better health. We want to know what to do next. We want reassurance that we can get better and we want to know our doctor will support us in that journey.

Similarly, the ultimate goal of classroom assessment is not to label students' strengths and weaknesses. The goal is to create a plan for growth. We want to provide students with the next steps and help them on the journey to becoming stronger mathematicians. Collecting data helps us understand where students are now, and more importantly, it helps us understand what students should do next.

Once teachers have conducted their data analysis, it is essential for teachers and students to act upon the data. As the saying goes, you don't fatten a pig by measuring it. Simply collecting data does not improve student achievement. The response to the data holds the potential for growth. What truly matters are the things teachers and students do as a result of what they learned from the classroom assessments. Once the data analysis has provided a clearer picture of what students currently know and what they are ready to learn next, it is time to intentionally design learning experiences to help each student move to that next step.

Students do not all learn the same way and at the same pace. The assessment data usually reflects that fact. After a typical assessment, many students will have demonstrated mastery over the content, while others show they are not there yet. When that assessment represents essential content that students need to know, teachers must take steps to support the group of students who have yet to achieve mastery.

Intervention is the process of providing additional instruction for specific students. There are a variety of reasons that students may need additional instruction:

- Students may simply need more time and additional practice with the content. For students who struggle with long-term memory storage and

DOI: 10.4324/9781003346333-20

retrieval, the rapid pace of the typical math classroom can make it challenging to learn the material at the same pace as their peers. Creating opportunities for spaced practice (returning to the content after a few days) can increase retention.

- Students may need help making sense of the content and connecting it to prior knowledge. Students find it more difficult to recall and apply knowledge and skills they have learned through rote processes. Effective mathematicians will form mental connections to link new learning to prior knowledge. These links can be unique to different students. Students with IEPs may have gaps in prior knowledge, meaning their mental links between math concepts may be very different from their peers. Teachers may find themselves individually analyzing some students' work in order to identify ways to make sense of the content. This may involve the use of math manipulatives, graphic organizers, or other forms of supplemental aids to help students make sense of the information they are learning.
- Students may hold misconceptions that need to be corrected. As students learn a wide range of skills in a short amount of time, it may not be clear how or when each skill should be applied. Students may think that only linear relationships have a rate of change or that the area of any figure can be calculated by multiplying two dimensions. Teachers can work to identify student misconceptions, then create learning experiences to directly address them. Manipulatives – virtual or concrete – can be helpful to make mathematical relationships visible and help students understand the underlying concepts at work.

Of course, there can also be other reasons students are struggling with math content. It is important to remember each student's developmental journey is unique. It is very rare that a one-size-fits-all, whole-class instructional approach will serve all students. Particularly when designing intervention – revisiting content after the initial instruction – teachers will usually benefit from deemphasizing whole-class approaches in favor of targeted instruction for specific groups of students based on their needs.

Whole-class approaches are attractive because they are simple and straightforward. Teachers can plan one task and assign it to the entire class. It can be tempting to assign the same review of material to all students. However, there are several drawbacks to this strategy. First, students will not all respond to instruction the same way. The initial instruction did not serve all students equally, so it is hard to imagine an intervention lesson that will truly benefit all students. Targeted, differentiated tasks will provide much better review and intervention. Further, reteaching material to an entire class when it is not necessary uses up valuable time in the instructional calendar. Math teachers often have more content to teach than they can comfortably fit into the school year, and class-wide reteach activities further cut into this time. Spaced practice and spiral reviews are absolutely appropriate, but intensive reteach lessons should be reserved for the specific groups of students who need them.

Students also perceive targeted interventions as a respectful task. They can see the connection between their current ability and the specific lessons designed to help them develop additional skills. This increases student engagement as they recognize the relevance of the task they are completing. This approach also encourages students to view assessments as a way to communicate with their teacher. They see that their assessments are used to shape future instruction, encouraging them to put forth their best effort on tests to truly reflect their ability. If students notice that the entire class is engaged in the same follow-up activity after a test, they may begin to lose respect for the process.

Early in my teaching career, after any classroom test, I would spend about half of a class period reviewing the test with my students. I would pass back graded tests and we would discuss three or four of the most missed items. I didn't reflect on this practice until I saw its impact on a particular student with Autism Spectrum Disorder (ASD). This student was very critical of himself and would become agitated anytime he received a low grade. Often when I returned his test paper, he would quickly tear it up or hide it in the trash can. Initially, this behavior irritated me because it disrupted my plans to occupy students by asking them to follow along on their own papers as we went over some of the test problems.

As I thought about how to adjust my plans to accommodate this student's needs, I began to realize this system of going over test questions helped very few of my students. Not everyone had missed the same questions, so when I chose the problems to address, many students found it to be a waste of their time. It certainly was not engaging to ask students to listen to me describe a solution strategy that I preferred. There was no consideration for the individual needs of my students.

I began finding alternate ways for students to address any areas of weakness their test revealed. Sometimes I placed students in heterogeneous groups and allowed them to discuss with each other how they approached test questions. Other times I pulled small groups of students to look at specific questions while the rest of the class was engaged in independent work. Two changes in my approach helped my student who used to tear up his tests (and I believe ultimately helped all of my students):

- My response to the test was more individualized and used fewer whole-class reviews. Students who showed mastery on the test could devote their class time to other skills they needed to practice. Students could continue working on as many areas of the test as necessary, often at their own pace.
- My response was less focused on the test and the items students missed and instead emphasized skills and knowledge students would need as they

progressed through the course content. Our conversations were less about how many students missed question number four and more about who still needed help finding the *y*-intercept from a table of values.

Some students with behavior or social issues may be particularly prone to frustration, like my student who tore up his test papers. Targeted interventions are a gentle way to encourage students with a low tolerance for criticism to self-evaluate their work. The intervention system is based on the idea that students can improve with proper support. Most students – not just students with IEPs – will need intervention on particular tasks at some point during the school year, reducing the stigma sometimes associated with review and retesting.

One approach to designing interventions is for teachers to list any issues they notice during the data analysis. Table 15.1 shows an example chart listing the learning target, the specific obstacle students exhibited, and the number of students who would benefit from this intervention. This list guides teachers as they design intervention tasks. It is often unreasonable for teachers to address all gaps and misconceptions in the days following an assessment, but this list helps teachers prioritize which issues to address first.

Table 15.1 Teachers may list learning gaps and misconceptions observed in the data analysis to prioritize planning intervention lessons

Learning Target	*Obstacle*	*No. of Students*
Students will identify the slope and *y*-intercept of a linear relationship from a table of values	**Difficulty:** Students did not correctly identify the slope from the table. **Task:** Practice identifying the change in *y* and the change in *x* from a table	6
	Difficulty: Students could not identify the *y*-intercept if it wasn't explicitly included in the table. **Task:** Use a graphic organizer to extend the table to find the *y*-intercept when the independent value is zero.	5
	Difficulty: Students tried graphing the points on the table, but plotted the points incorrectly. **Task:** Review identifying points on the coordinate plane	2
Students will write an equation to represent a linear relationship given the slope and the *y*-intercept	**Difficulty:** Students wrote an equation in slope-intercept form that did not have the given slope or *y*-intercept. **Task:** Practice verifying that the equation matches the graph by graphing	4

One of the challenges of targeted interventions is making sure that all students are engaged in meaningful, relevant math work. If teachers do not use a whole-class review strategy, they must find or create different assignments for different groups of students. If students move ahead to the next unit, that may extend learning gaps and make differentiation after the next assessment even more challenging. However, students who do not need intervention on the material from this assessment can review prior material or explore the content more deeply through some extension activities.

Intervention should always include new instruction. It is not adequate to encourage students to reread their notes or correct their tests. If teachers believe that a test accurately measures what their students know, then it is essential for students to participate in new experiences that will increase their knowledge before they are assessed again. That learning experience can look different depending on the learning target and the particular student. Teachers may create an interactive task, facilitate some guided practice, or simply engage in a small group question-and-answer session to correct student misconceptions.

Students should only be required to receive new instruction on the skills and concepts they have not mastered. If time allows, students can certainly opt in to any reteach that interests them, but assigning students to intervention should be directly tied to students' current level of understanding. Again, teachers should avoid whole-class interventions whenever reasonable. Additionally, students with memory or attention issues often benefit from chunked tasks. Focusing only on select portions of an assessment is a powerful way to help students avoid feeling overwhelmed by the work in front of them.

Teachers should notice that intervention is also an opportunity to implement SDI for students with IEPs. Reteach will often provide an opportunity to address a student's IEP goals. Teachers should look for ways that IEP goal strategies – such as graphic organizers, supplemental aids, sentence stems, etc. – can be applied to the assessment skills and concepts that students need to strengthen. When IEP goals and instructional goals align, it is a perfect opportunity to support students.

In one particularly high-functioning PLC I worked with, teachers committed to examining student work during the unit on the Pythagorean theorem, and the impact was immediate. The first assessment asked students to calculate the length of a right triangle's side, and after the assessments, teachers each brought in a few sample test papers to discuss. The teachers noted that most students were doing well with the topic, answering most of the questions correctly. When they turned their attention to the struggling students' papers, they quickly noticed a theme. The most common difficulties showed up when problems contained only text and no diagram. Several students were having trouble distinguishing when they should be solving for the hypotenuse of a right triangle and when they should calculate the length of one of the triangle's legs. In the group of struggling students, most students did not draw any sort of diagram, and those who did mislabeled the triangles' dimensions.

The teachers created a task to directly address this issue. Students were given a set of cards that contained only the text of 12 different right triangle problems. Students were asked to match these cards with another set of cards that each contained a diagram of one of the triangles described on the problem cards. During the task, teachers checked students' work and helped students articulate the strategies they were using to match the cards. Brief conversations with students allowed teachers to insert academic vocabulary common to right triangle problems, such as hypotenuse, right angle, and even compass directions. After students correctly matched the cards, students were given three new problems and asked to draw their own diagram for each problem before calculating the length of the missing dimension.

Following this reteach task, students in the intervention group were retested and teachers examined the new results. They found the intervention was effective for many students. Most of the retest group now mastered the skill, and when the teachers examined the papers of students who were still struggling, they identified a new problem. Only a few students still needed help, and their papers showed that all these students did not understand how to calculate the square root of a number – an essential skill in most right triangle problems that rely on the Pythagorean theorem. The students who still struggled seemed to believe they could divide a number by two to determine its square root.

The teachers developed another intervention task for these few remaining students. They practiced finding the areas of squares from the length of a side, then working backward to determine the side length when given the area. After students had observed that the side length of a square was not usually half of its area, the students applied that knowledge to using the Pythagorean theorem.

This group of teachers had agreed their eighth-grade students must know how to use the Pythagorean theorem to calculate the length of a right triangle's side. They felt the skill had some practical applications and they believed the skill also prepared students for future coursework where they would need to solve equations for a variable or calculate the distance between points on the coordinate plane. Since the teachers believed this skill was important, they persisted in working with students until the students achieved mastery. The teachers examined student work to identify specific obstacles, designed lessons to improve students' understanding of the mathematics, and then re-evaluated students' abilities.

This approach can be challenging. These teachers were able to implement their intervention lessons as short pull-out stations in their classes while they continued addressing new content, but finding time for intervention can be difficult. Depending on the campus culture, teachers may leverage tutoring times outside of class or video lessons. The most effective way to capture all students is to implement interventions during normal class time. Most students have some skills that should be working to improve, so teachers can often find meaningful tasks for each student to work on during intervention times.

Conducting differentiated, targeted interventions often involves several moving parts. Students are not all working on the same task at the same time and at the same pace. A few logistical tips can help interventions run more smoothly and help students get used to the process. When class members are engaged in different tasks, it is important that each student knows what they should be doing. Particularly for students with IEPs, it is helpful to display this information visually. This allows students to refer back to the information if they need help self-monitoring their progress, forget their instructions, or struggle to pay attention to a list of directions.

First, it is important to clearly communicate which task(s) are assigned to each student. Consider a scenario where students recently completed a test covering two different skills. This usually means the teacher will provide a task reviewing task #1, a task reviewing task #2, and a separate task #3 for students who do not need (or have already completed) these reviews. Each task should be meaningful and engaging. Students should not feel they are being punished with a task that is "less fun" than others. Here are a few sample ways to tell each student their assignments:

- Display a class-wide spreadsheet showing each student's name or initials and the order of tasks they should complete. Teachers can implement an element of student choice by asking students to complete the first task in their list, then choose any additional tasks next to their name. It is important that each student has tasks to complete and that intervention is presented to the class in a way to prevent any stigma.
- Provide each student with an individual printout listing their assigned tasks. This requires a little more preparation but provides greater student privacy. Students can keep this list in a folder to refer to over multiple days of intervention.
- Assign tasks through a digital Learning Management System (LMS). Many LMS platforms such as Google Classroom, Schoology, or Canvas provide ways for teachers to send assignments to individual students. Teachers can send students the actual assignments or an ordered list of tasks.

Once students know *which* tasks to complete, teachers must then communicate *what* to do. Students may be able to complete some tasks independently while teachers need to facilitate others. It is normal to see two classroom stations where students are working with each other, receiving occasional help from their teacher while a third group of students is working directly with their teacher receiving new instruction. Students who struggle with listening comprehension often have trouble following a long list of directions. Chunking directions into two or three instructions at a time may be helpful. Posting instructions at the station or at the top of the page can also be helpful. This allows students to easily refer to the instructions without disrupting the teacher who may be helping other students.

Classes should develop a protocol for requesting help from the teacher. If students are working in groups, teachers may instruct students to ask their group members for help before asking the teacher. Groups may institute a signal to get the teacher's attention, such as placing a colored card on their table or displaying a colored sticky note. Students can display a green card if things are going well, a yellow card to ask for help when the teacher is available, and a red card to indicate they need help as soon as possible.

Each of these protocols is intended to help manage the variety of activities that happen during the targeted, differentiated intervention. Though intervention may require some additional preparation, the benefit to student learning is significant. Since interventions are providing each student with instruction and practice on the exact skills they need to develop, it is usually acceptable for a set of intervention tasks to last for multiple days, helping to decrease the amount of preparation teachers must undertake.

In one sense, when teachers respond to assessment data, they are starting the lesson cycle all over again. Examining student work provides new insight into strengths and weaknesses. Teachers begin crafting new learning targets based on what students are ready to learn next and designing targeted instruction to address specific students' needs. That instruction is adapted to the specific student and teachers monitor and facilitate the learning. Finally, students are re-assessed and the cycle is ready to repeat.

For students with IEPs, this learning journey will look different from many of their peers, but they still have the right to access rich, meaningful math goals. It is helpful to consider unique student needs during each part of the lesson cycle – as teachers craft learning targets, deliver instruction, design assessments, analyze data, and provide interventions. This student-centered approach will improve student achievement and better prepare them for future coursework and success beyond school.